INSECURE

ATTACHMENT

ANXIOUS OR AVOIDANT IN LOVE? HOW ATTACHMENT STYLES HELP OR HURT YOUR RELATIONSHIPS.

LEARN TO FORM SECURE EMOTIONAL CONNECTIONS

DAVID LAWSON PHD

© **Copyright 2020 by David Lawson PhD- All rights reserved.**

The content contained within this book may not be reproduced, duplicated or transmitted without direct written permission from the author or the publisher.

Under no circumstances will any blame or legal responsibility be held against the publisher, or author, for any damages, reparation, or monetary loss due to the information contained within this book; either directly or indirectly.

Legal Notice:

This book is copyright protected. This book is only for personal use. You cannot amend, distribute, sell, use, quote or paraphrase any part, or the content within this book, without the consent of the author or publisher.

Disclaimer Notice:

Please note the information contained within this document is for educational and entertainment purposes only. All effort has been executed to present accurate, up-to-date, and reliable, complete information. No warranties of any kind are declared or implied. Readers acknowledge that the author is not engaging in the rendering of legal, financial, medical or professional advice.

TABLE OF CONTENTS

Introduction 1

Chapter 1: How Childhood Affects Life 7

Chapter 2: The 3 Different Insecure Attachment Types 15

Chapter 3: Facts Attachment Bonding 22

Chapter 4: How Insecure Attachment Affects Your Love Style 29

Chapter 5: Attachment and Friendship 36

Chapter 6: Dating and Insecure Attachment 44

Chapter 7: How To Find Your Partner 50

Chapter 8: How To Feel Good Without a Relationship................... 57

Chapter 9: Dealing With Insecure Attachment Issues 65

Chapter 10: The New Skills You Need To Learn 72

Chapter 11: Change Your Behavior... 79

Chapter 12: How To Heal Your Attachment Wounds..................... 86

Conclusion 91

INTRODUCTION

Are your most essential qualities and behaviors determined by your genetics or are they learned? This is the most enduring debate of our times.

The modern scientific view is that the capacity to behave in a specific way is genetic, but experiences will determine how, when, and whether these capacities are engaged.

As attachment is about how distress is managed, the answer would lie in how often distress is experienced. How it is expressed lies in the genetic factors, but the responses to stress are modified by learning and experiences. Thus, how an infant develops an attachment style is mostly learned.

Early relationships with parents and caregivers certainly do shape what you expect from and how you participate in later relationships, specifically in romantic attachments. You develop a blueprint of how you interact in adult relationships, how you seek comfort or push it away, how you trust or don't, and how you approach any situation that could be perceived as a conflict.

However, other relationships and circumstances in your formative years, as well as later relationships, also play a big role.

For a relationship to be successful, people need to be secure. This means they need to govern their emotions and habits in order to ensure a peaceful coexistence with their partner. Partners need to be well-adjusted in order to have a healthy and rewarding relationship. But sadly, this cannot be said to be the case for many relationships. Partners that struggle with insecure attachment issues are virtually incapable of having healthy relationships. Psychologists believe that insecure attachment begins in early childhood. The experiences of a child in relation to their parents and the surrounding environment are going to influence how they turn out as adults. When a child develops a healthy bond with the people in their early life, they become secure. This means they will have a positive attitude and expect the best from other people. Such kids grow to be solid partners who expect other people to play their part. But when a child has an unhealthy bond with their early life environment, such a kid is likely to grow up to exhibit insecure attachment, whereby they expect the worst of people. Such people end up becoming distrustful of others and this presents significant challenges in relationships. They are likely to be unpredictable. They won't show any consistency in their behaviors and actions. One moment they might act charged and interested and the next moment they might act withdrawn and disconnected, like a robot. Insecure attachment may be overcome but it requires the full participation of the affected person. This book delves into the subject of insecure attachment issues and makes suggestions on how to get rid of it.

Relationships play a critical role in our happiness, but if the partners are not compatible, it can give rise to tremendous pain. One of the factors that contributes to difficult relationships is the presence of insecure attachment issues in either or both partners. Generally, attachment issues stem from an individual's childhood experiences. If the child had a stable relationship with their parents, they developed a healthy bond with other human beings, and in later years when they get into a relationship, they will have a positive mindset and expect to rely on the other person. However, if someone had a negative relationship with their parent, they likely developed an unhealthy bond, and it makes it hard for them to trust their partners; these people will always be expecting their partners to do them in and this mindset usually sabotages the relationship.

Relationships are hard. That's a common truth.

You might think that learning how to spend large amounts of time with another person, perhaps live with another person, and co-exist beside them would be easy, after all, we're all human, right?

Wrong.

Learning how to compromise, communicate, overcome conflict, express your emotions, and trust is extremely difficult. We're not born to be in relationships naturally, it's something we have to adapt and learn.

You might think that we're making the world of love sound like a course you need to take at college, with a rather tough exam at the end, but ask yourself this – if relationships were easy, would we be talking about them all the time? Would there be so many glossy magazines with articles dedicated to them? Would we have chat shows bemoaning relationship issues?

No, we would simply allow relationships to fit into our lives, perhaps in the same way that we do with Netflix.

A successful relationship takes hard work, compromise, and trust, but those three things aren't easy to come by in this day and age. The number of couples with trust issues is staggering, and that could be down to previous infidelity or simple paranoia because of the amount of social media used by one side of the partnership.

No, relationships aren't easy, but they're more than worth the hard work.

If you're someone who finds love hard, worry no more. You're not alone, and you're certainly not in the minority. It's important to be comfortable, yourself, secure and happy in any relationship that you enter into, but come on, that's easier said than done!

Love is supposed to be calm, happy, and uplifting, but sometimes it is so riddled with anxiety problems that it can become a chore, every single day you're with that person.

If you want to rid yourself of relationship anxiety, the first step is recognizing where it's coming from and acknowledging that it is playing a part in your life.

The road towards happiness and security in love starts with yourself. Nobody can fix a problem for you, but we can help you identify where the issue comes from and give you the best advice to overcome it.

We're not going to preach, we're not going to judge, and we're not going to tell you that with a little hard thinking you can fix any problem that comes your way. What we are going to do is show you that the future can be a lot brighter than it is now, and you can find your way towards a happy, healthy, and secure relationship in the very near future.

As humans, we have an in-built desire to connect with others. This helps us feel needed, part of something bigger than ourselves, and it also makes us feel loved. Of course, nobody NEEDS a partner to be complete – that is something else entirely. What we're talking about here is the human desire to be a part of a union.

You might meet the odd person who simply doesn't want to be in a relationship. That's fine, but what you will probably find with people such as this, is that they seek out friendship connections instead. We all need people in our lives; it helps us feel happier, healthier, and more hopeful for the future. Loneliness is one of the biggest causes of depression, and we all know about the dark road that depression leads you down.

It's no surprise that one of the best self-help methods for managing depression is to surround yourself with people who you love and care about, those who lift you up and do their best to raise your spirits. This is simply because the bonding hormones that are released by our brains when we're close to others gives us a natural high.

Think about the first few times you met your partner. Did you get butterflies when you saw them? Did you think about them constantly? That's your brain kicking out oxytocin and other 'bonding' hormones, helping you to feel connected to another person. It almost feels like an addiction, because you feel happy and content whenever you're near them and you miss them when they're gone.

Of course, this tapers off after a while, but by that time the closeness has been developed differently.

Put simply, relationships help us to be a better version of ourselves. They help us to open up and be vulnerable, to risk it all for love and give us the opportunity to love someone else unconditionally. Love is beautiful, but it can also be extremely rocky and difficult from time to time!

The point we need to make here is that you should never feel like you have to be in a relationship to be "whole." The only person who can make you whole is yourself but sharing your life with another person brings a whole new dimension of happiness and contentment. This person becomes part of your family, and your relationship evolves over time. At first, it's all honeymoons and stars, and it eventually cools down and turns into true companionship as the years pass by.

Relationships are beautiful, but you should never stay in the wrong one either. Remember, you don't NEED a relationship, but if you want one, you need to understand what not to do and how not to feel, to keep it as beautiful as it is intended to be.

CHAPTER 1
HOW CHILDHOOD AFFECTS LIFE

The experiences that we have as children can play a critical role in how we turn out. If we had a terrible childhood, we are likely to grow up maladjusted. For most people with insecure attachment issues, childhood abuse is one of the major causes. Children are extremely vulnerable and the emotional or physical hurt that they experience comes to haunt them much later. The following are some of the experiences that can be traumatic for children.

Domestic violence

In some dysfunctional homes, parents can be cruel. It normally starts with them going for each other, but soon enough they start focusing on their kids. Kids who have been physically abused tend to endure a lot of trauma, and once they become young adults, they exhibit various issues including insecure attachment. Domestic violence leaves the kid forever scarred as they remember the pain they endured at the hands of their parent or guardian.

Abandonment

Kids are vulnerable. They need to grow up in the warmth of loving parents. But some kids are unfortunate in the sense that they have parents who couldn't care less. Their parents might be emotionally distant or have a tendency of leaving them for long periods. It never turns out well. Kids need to have both parents around so that they can become emotionally stable. For kids who are struggling with abandonment issues, it becomes increasingly hard for them to adjust to society, and it gives rise to a number of mental health issues.

Sexual abuse

This is probably one of the worst things for a kid to endure. Kids who are sexually abused tend to have a hard time fitting into society. This is because sexual violence tends to destroy a person's emotional stability. The trauma that comes about as a result of sexual abuse is unrivaled. It is life-long too. The person might seek help and all of that but still they will feel haunted by memories of what happened to them. Subjecting a kid to sexual abuse is quite simply ruining their life.

Verbal abuse

Another experience that sends a kid into trauma is verbal abuse. This usually happens when one or both of their parents are mentally unstable. In most cases, the verbally abusive parent tends to come from a place of being hurt themselves. But two wrongs don't make a right. It doesn't matter that they were hurt too, but they should have the sense to stop the cycle of hurt and start treating their kids with more respect. Verbal abuse makes a kid deeply resentful. It affects their self-esteem and causes them to have a hard time fitting into society. They also develop insecure attachment issues.

Loss of a loved one

At the end of the day, we are just mortals. We inevitably have to leave this planet. But the problem is that some people leave the planet whilst having dependents. When a kid loses their loved one, particularly their parent, they can have a hard time adjusting in society, because they no longer have the necessary emotional stability. Loss of a loved one can cause a kid to have a terrible attitude too, because they have the wrong impression of the world; they think that the world is out to get them, and it can send them on the wrong path.

Accidents

Another experience that could send a kid into trauma is an accident. The more technologically advanced we are, the more machines we have to operate, and the more risk we subject ourselves to. If a kid is involved in an accident, for instance, a road accident, they could be scarred for life, because they have no conception of how to process the events. It might cause them to develop a negative attitude toward life because they are afraid of the next tragedy.

Life-threatening illnesses

Thank heavens we are at a stage where we have eliminated most medical problems from the planet. But there are still many illnesses still left. A kid who is battling some form of illness is in a world of pain and they can be left traumatized for the rest of their life. Kids are very aware of what's going on. Being ill stops them from being a normal kid. It gets in the way of their fun. It causes them to have a negative outlook on life.

Natural disasters

As we continue to burden Mother Earth with our mindless activities, nature will find ways of striking back, and you better be sure that when Mother Earth strikes back, there's a large trail of destruction. One of the common ways that Mother Earth strikes back is through hurricanes. They hit coastal cities and bring the buildings down. Kids who witness that are left traumatized for the rest of their life. Various emotional issues, including insecure attachment issues, can stem from such a traumatic experience.

Refugee experience

Again, the world is in relative political stability, but still there are people in certain corners of the world who are still fighting. Kids who are native to such places and have to be carried away as refugees have a hard time developing emotional stability. Refugee camps cannot provide the warmth that a kid is entitled to.

Bullying

Kids are sweet, but they can also be nasty, especially against their fellow children. Bullying can start in the early schooling years and can last until high school. But it leaves the target devastated. Kids who have been bullied could have a hard time fitting in and developing the emotional stability necessary to become self-sufficient. They could develop insecure attachment issues that make it difficult for them to have normal relationships.

Fear

When a child is going through a traumatic experience, the first response they have is fear. They exhibit signs of terror as they feel threatened. For instance, if a child is undergoing bullying at school, they might not always disclose it, because they are embarrassed about what they are going through, but they will always appear scared for their life. You can spot the fear in their eyes, in their hesitation, and they will be extra careful about what they say or do.

Anxiety

Anxiety starts pretty early. When a child is experiencing anxiety, it is usually as a result of the traumatic experience that they are going through. For instance, if a kid has just lost their parent, they look around and see that their momma or dad is not around anymore, and they just feel anxious. Nothing ever feels the same anymore. They are looking for ways to express their pain but they can't even conceptualize it. Their anxiety stops them from becoming well-adjusted. It stops them from being happy. They cannot fit in among other kids. And this is painful.

Depression

Also, kids can be depressed. It usually occurs when a kid is going through a traumatic experience. They don't have the emotional stability to process their feelings and make sense of what is happening in their life, and so, they shut off. Most kids who are depressed have a tendency to hide themselves. They don't want to spend time with their friends or their family, and they always keep to themselves. And this makes it hard for them to have an easy time. Depressed kids will also have antisocial tendencies, and in the quiet of their room, they might weep.

Nightmares

Dreams are a way for our subconscious to make sense of various things in our life. Kids who are going through a traumatic time will experience nightmares regularly. These nightmares will keep them awake because they are in the middle of making sense of what is happening to them. If you notice that a kid is struggling with nightmares, it might be an indication that they are going through a traumatic experience. Also, it is not a good sign when a kid has difficulties falling asleep; it means that they too are having traumas.

Loss of appetite

As kids are constantly growing, they require a lot of energy, and this is made clear through their massive appetites. So, it's a bad sign when a kid is not eating enough. It indicates that the kid is going through a traumatic experience. For instance, when a kid runs into bullies at school and keeps quiet about it, you might notice them first withdrawing, and then they will begin to lose their appetite. Kids are supposed to have an appetite because their body needs a lot of nutrition. Thus, it might be a sign of trauma when a kid won't indulge in food with enthusiasm.

Trouble forming relationships

Another clear sign that a child is going through trauma is an inability to form relationships with other people. This is usually driven by their anxiety and fears. Relationships play an important role in our lives and failure to form meaningful relationships is also a bad sign. The kid is against forming any relationships with other people because they have developed the wrong outlook on life; they think that human beings are not to be trusted, that human beings only bring trouble, and therefore human beings need to be shunned.

Inability to trust anyone

When a kid experiences trauma at the hands of an individual, especially their parent, they will come away thinking that human beings at large mean them harm, and they will make a point of avoiding every last human being, or at least not trust them ever again. And this is one of the reasons why it's hard for them to have any meaningful relationship with other people. A kid who has deep trust issues tends to be a loner, because only then they are in charge of the whole process, and they can rely on themselves.

Difficulty concentrating

Another indicator that a kid is going through a traumatic experience is an inability to concentrate. They tend to have a faraway look, because they are lost thinking about the trauma they are experiencing, and it is quite hard for them to overcome this pain.

Poor academic performance

When a kid is going through trauma, they will have a difficult time concentrating on their education, and they will score poor grades. Also, they will have difficulties comprehending whatever they are learning because most of their mental energy goes toward processing the traumatic experiences they are going through.

Risky behavior

In most cases, trauma tends to overwhelm kids and makes them quiet. But then there are cases where kids react to trauma by going overboard. Such kids will start indulging in risky behaviors as a way to forget their traumatic experiences. Of course, such behaviors only prepare them for the path of delinquency and more often than not it ends badly.

Aches

Some kids react to traumatic experiences through feeling pain in certain areas of their body. This can be especially unnerving because kids need to be in great physical health so they can enjoy their early childhood.

People who have insecure attachment issues are likely to have gone through a traumatic experience in early childhood. It may get worse depending on whether or not anyone comes to their aid.

CHAPTER 2
THE 3 DIFFERENT INSECURE ATTACHMENT TYPES

Different ways of communicating and participating in relationships describe attachment styles. Attachment models concentrate on how children and parents communicate during early childhood. Commitment types are used in adulthood to identify patterns of commitment in romantic relationships. The theory and attachment studies that emerged throughout the 1960s and 1970s developed the concept of attachment styles. Psychologists today usually recognize four significant styles of attachment.

What is attachment?

Attachment is an emotional relationship involving an exchange of warmth, treatment and enjoyment. The study of attachment began with Freud's love theories, but as a father of attachment theory, another writer is generally cited.

John Bowlby has devoted extensive research to the concept of attachment, describing it as a "lasting psychological connection between humans."

Bowlby shared the psychoanalytic view that experiences of early childhood are important for later life to influence development and behavior. Our early styles of attachment are established in childhood through the baby-caregiver relationship.

In addition, Bowlby believed that attachment had an evolutionary component; help in survival. "The propensity to establish strong emotional ties with particular individuals [is] a basic component of human nature," he explained.

Disorganized/disoriented attachment

Disorganized attachment is recognized as a serious predictor of maladjustment and psychopathology in children. (Benoit, 2004)

Disorganized attachment puts children at risk for lack of control of emotions, stress, hostile and aggressive behaviors and coercive styles of interactions. They lack self-esteem and confidence, are rejected by their peers and struggle academically, especially in mathematics.

At an early age they:

Show a mix of avoidant and resistant behaviors

May seem dizzy, confused or apprehensive

At six years old:

Can take on a parental role

Some children may act as careers for their parents.

Children with an unsafe and unorganized attachment style demonstrate a lack of clear attachment behavior. These children are described as exhibiting stunning behavior, sometimes appearing confused or apprehensive in the presence of a caregiver.

Main and Solomon proposed that inconsistent parenting behavior could be a contributing factor to this attachment style. As the child feels both comforted and frightened by the parents, it results in confusion.

The young child has conflicting, inconsistent and often frustrating behaviors in this type of attachment. For example, they can cling to the attachment as they look away or weep when he leaves without closing. These behaviors seem incomprehensible and show that a coherent attachment strategy is lacking in construction.

Anxious-ambivalent attachment

In this case, we have a child who learns very early that he cannot trust his parents. Sometimes, they show some affection, others are cold and distant.

They are fathers and mothers who oscillate between times of abandonment or neglect and moments of severity and control. All this generates ambivalent situations in which the child lives in a state of constant anxiety and insecurity. He has little or no control over what happens, so he doesn't know what to expect; an uncertainty that does not know how to manage and that only generates insecurity.

Attachment styles and emotional memory tell us that the person, in this case, ends up focusing on certain events of the past. For example, the adult will remember those moments of the past in which he needed support or help and did not receive it, moments in which he felt alone, scared...

It creates, therefore, an "attachment" to those unresolved and painful issues, from which, in some way, rage and frustration are fed even more. They are emotions that tend to block the person, hence, it is often difficult for them to also release each memory, each painful experience.

In ambivalent attachment, the attachment sometimes provides care behaviors, and sometimes they do not. It is this insecurity that causes children to not want to explore the world since they do not know if when they ask for help, their demands will be answered or not.

This type of ambivalent attachment gives rise to people who, in relationships, do not know how to deal with their problems autonomously. In addition, they are people who direct their attention to anxiety and fear and compulsively seek that attention and help.

As children they:

- May be wary of strangers
- Be very distressed when parents leave
- Don't look comforted when parents return

As adults they:

- •Are reluctant to approach others
- •Worry their partner doesn't love them
- •Become very upset when relationships end

According to Cassidy and Berlin, the attachment of twins is relatively rare, and this attachment style is demonstrated by only 7% to 15% of US babies. As these children grow up, teachers often describe them as overly dependent and dependent.

For adults, those with an ambivalent style of relationship are often hesitant to engage others and are worried that their partner will not reciprocate their feelings. This leads to frequent breakups, mostly due to the cold and distant relationship. Some people feel especially distressed after a marriage breakup. Cassidy and Berlin identified another pattern of pathology in which ambivalent adults cling to young children as a source of protection.

Anxious-avoidant attachment

In this case, avoidance attachment appears when a child assimilates, even if not consciously, that his need for care will be answered with indifference, if not with contempt. This means that, generally, these children try to become emotionally self-sufficient people.

Thus, in order to not experience more damage, emptiness or suffering, they choose to shape an emotional detachment that will characterize much of their relationships.

Studies, like the aforementioned, indicate that in these cases it is common to create gaps, disjointed or fragmented memories. Many childhood episodes are forgotten or remembered inaccurately.

Interestingly, people characterized by avoidance attachment in their emotional relationships also exhibit memory problems.

Forgetting probably facilitates their emotional detachment from the people around them. As a hypothesis, we can think that it is a defense mechanism that ends up causing the brain itself to lower the intensity of suffering at the cost of raising the sensitivity threshold.

As we can see, attachment styles and emotional memory share a direct link. The quality of our early relationships mediates the quality of our emotional life. Thus, if a past of traumatic experiences is hidden behind the door of our present, it is necessary to cross that threshold to resolve and heal that universe.

Avoidant attachment arises when the caregiver does not respond to the child's demands for care. Therefore, and since they have not become accustomed to that, these children do not seek their caregivers when exploring the world; they don't seem to exist to them.

Relationships that arise as a result of an avoidant attachment are elusive. The signs of anxiety and fear of the couple are not attended to, and neither is their help sought when one feels that fear or needs care. Such care is not requested and does not seek social support to solve problems.

At the time of separation, the insecure, avoiding child does not turn to his attachment and tries to mask his emotional distress by detachment from the situation and the physical environment. He pretends to be indifferent or avoids contact with his caregiver by remaining more focused on his toys. A. Guedeney and N. Guedeney (2002) state that in the first interactions between the baby and his caregiver, the latter appears to be detached and not very available to meet the needs of his child. The young child does not seem to be able to develop a basis of security in relation to his mother and this can give an impression of early independence.

Insecure avoiding behavior has been observed in young whiny children, who tend to panic during the separation from their caregiver and who, on their return reject it with rage without showing any sign of relief. In an experimental situation, insecure avoiding children would be the ones who display the most emotions and anxiety, which would cause the deactivation of their attachment system in order to better manage this situation. In this context, the young child stands out, shows little emotion, turns more towards exploration and is forced to adopt early autonomy as a survival strategy.

Hopkins (1992), referring to Mr. Ainsworth's analyses, explains that avoidant attachment strategies refer to the failure of the holding company. This is what Mr. Ainsworth calls 'rejection syndrome' for mothers who show a deep aversion to physical contact. The strategies of this type of attachment thus take on a defensive value and an adaptation function in the face of a rejecting environment.

In adults, this type of attachment results in a detached attachment style. The individual describes himself as uncomfortable in an intimate and deep relationship as well as anxious in situations of closeness. According to Hazan and Shaver (1987), the detached subject perceives the relationship with others as threatening proximity, because it risks arousing the archaic fear of being rejected by the significant person. These individuals have self-confidence, but not confidence in others, which makes them avoid intimate relationships. Tarabulsy states that there are 17% of adults in the general population who suffer this type of attachment.

CHAPTER 3
FACTS ATTACHMENT BONDING

The attachment of an infant to a significant caregiver is the most momentous event in the growth of the child's personality. It is the source of the feeling of safety, self-esteem, and self-control of the child. However, the impact of a first connection goes far beyond emotion. It affects how well the kid remembers, knows, and gets along with others. A stable connection (or its weakness or absence) wires the brain of a child in a set pattern.

How can an early childhood aspect hold so much power over a lifetime? And how do children's psychologists know about attachment? This segment responds to both questions.

More than 50 years ago, John Bowlby (1907-1990) completed his naturalistic observations of adolescents, and subsequent research only reinforced his views among psychologists. Bowlby was a British psychiatrist and a professional psychoanalyst who acknowledged Freud's basic understanding of the importance of early childhood interaction in personality development. Bowlby applied to Freudianism a detailed analysis of the particular experiences that create a safe and precarious first relationship between a mother and her child. And he draws on ethology to establish the organizational theory in order to explain how these relationships derive from mother and child's instincts for survival.

It's in your smile. How can anyone resist a face like that? A baby's smile and kewpie's cheeks are actually irresistible for many adults. Bowlby indicated how this visual charm works as a brilliant adaptation (not unlike kittens, birds, or cowboys) to ensure a baby's way is almost essential for its affection, comfort, and food. The inherent actions of a mother to support and protect her newborn are generally enough to make her a part of this very mutual relationship.

Babies have a wide range of highly effective cues in what Bowlby called the "human attachment system" to ensure they get what they need to survive and thrive. If they are not laughing, they weep and fuss or coo and grab the lips, hair, and breasts of their mother. They watch her every step around the house as a duckling follows its mother through the grass.

Babies are social by the age of three months, but they usually save their biggest smile for the significant caregiver in their lives. In naming these behaviors adaptive, Bowlby pointed out that they were innate. The baby's target, he said, is to remain close to the primary source of his independent survival.

Bowlby found that new hatched chicks and ducklings create a unique process called "imprinting" for the first moving object that they see. Similar to these birds, human newborns prefer moving objects and often remember their mothers within days of birth. However, full binding on the part of a human baby takes at least six months longer than other species of animals. Luckily, human parents fail to get any slack in the bonding process. After a few minutes with a newborn, moms and fathers usually say that they were goners, already "in love."

Attachment to a primary caregiver is usually formed by the sixth or seventh month of a baby's life. Bowlby noticed in another bow to ethology that this timeframe coincides with the beginning of a crawling baby. This suggested a link between independent movement and the baby's completion of the attachment process that began at birth. For example, a kid takes a lot more time to get out of his crib than a chick does to fly out of his egg. Before kids are able to wander too far, instinct makes sure they know where to find "home base."

The two competing objectives in the earliest years of a baby are security and exploration. A child that remains secure survives; a child that explores the intelligence and skills necessary to grow successfully. Both of these needs often stand against each other. Bowlby and his predecessors, therefore, assume that a child develops an inner "thermostat" in order to monitor his environmental safety. An internal alarm bell sounds when he gets too far from home.

It is a common phenomenon that when a kid is leaving his mother (either by walking or "toddling") he will turn around to see if his mother is still close at hand. Maybe he will keep going if she's where he left her. Or he might come back to the base before his exploration restarts. The attachment bonding process allows children to control their desire to explore or stick to that particular person by internalizing what Bowlby called their caregiver's working models. "Mom's going to go there if you go farther." One model might be "It's too scary you shouldn't go too far," so babies form one model, or another based on the behavior of their mothers over time.

Striking photos of some very sad, even self-destructive monkeys persuaded many of the doubters of the value of the early animal and human mother-child bonding in the 1950s. These pictures come from the famous series of Rhesus monkey experiments. One was made of bare wire, and the other was covered in a soft cloth beneath the wire.

INSECURE ATTACHMENT

The baby monkeys developed a connection, but only with the cloth-covered cables, not the exposed cable. Interestingly, both kinds of substitutes supplied food via a bottle attached to the wire. It shows the scientists that the connection between the child and its caregiver is not solely based on the menu. There was another thing behind the bonding.

In Harlow's experiments, baby monkeys usually clung to the cloth-covered wire "mothers," in a striking manner similar to how they clung to a real monkey mother. The experiment demonstrated convincingly that the critical ingredient in attachment formation is not food but "contact comfort."

The findings of Harlow altered the psychoanalysis of how mother-child bonds are formed, making physical contact from skin to skin as important as a newborn baby's oral satisfaction during their mother's nursing or bottle feeding. Harlow's study also opposed the position of conductual theorists, who emphasized food itself as the primary strengthener of a baby's behavior.

Harlow's Rhesus monkey trials powerfully revealed that grave adverse consequences occur when a human baby in the first year of his life is deprived of a strong bond with a mother. Bowlby then confirmed that hypothesis by observing children in orphanages after the Second World War.

Many lessons gleaned from such studies concerned the long-term adverse effects of this deprivation on the emotional and physical wellbeing of the monkeys. In order to compensate a missing mother, these monkeys would suck their own bodies obsessively. They stayed in corners and rocked with a distant look in their eyes. Later, they became hostile, aggressive, and rarely mated with other monkeys. Later experiments on other monkeys helped clarify the importance of timing for patterns of human mother-baby attachment. Monkeys who had been with their mothers for at least three months before being separated exhibited fewer behavioral abnormalities than those that had been separated from birth. At six months of age, Monkeys separated from their mothers showed no long-term negative behavior. Researchers found that the attachment period among mothers and baby monkeys is crucial and will last for six months. In humans, it is estimated that this critical period lasts three years, with any deprivation most harmful in the first year of life.

Even with mothers' and babies' instincts and parental awe, attachment is not a direct method that begins and ends in the maternity ward. It is more like a dance that starts before birth and lasts for the first year of a baby's life. While the mother is usually the primary object of a baby's attachment, it's also likely that anyone who provides consistent and affectionate baby support – whether his father, grandparent, or adoptive parent – will have the same secure attachment to the baby. Factors that increase safe attachment include:

One baby primary, regular caregiver, rather than a series of irregular caregivers for the first six months of the year.

Synchronized feeding, sleeping, and stimulation routines with this caregiver, especially during the first few months of a baby's life.

The primary caregiver's constant smile, touch, and love.

They are consistently behaving with ease, warmth, and integrity in response to the baby's distress.

The responsiveness of a caregiver to the distress of a baby is necessary, but too much is counterproductive. Research shows that, when super-attentive mothers immediately reacted to the screams and hiccups of their babies, their children became less secure. The lesson is that children respond poorly to smothering. This hampers their freedom and hampers the cycle of self-soothing learning.

The attachment chemistry, the biochemistry behind parent-baby bonding, is a further perspective for attachment. Using brain scans and hormone levels and heart rate testing, researchers can now see the biochemical results when a safe attachment is produced, and when it is not carried out.

A woman's hormones prepare her for conception, and then make her nurse and nurture a newborn baby. Her brain circuits will be rewired during pregnancy, and her senses will be adapted to the additional physical and emotional demands of caring for a newborn. Because of her evolutionary instincts in this intense preparation of chemistry for birth, she will focus almost all of her attention and energy on this small person until its survival is secured.

The hormone oxytocin is essential throughout the animal kingdom for the first mother-child bonding that happens after a baby's birth. Much of the knowledge of the role of this hormone in human relations is based on animal studies. Female rats and sheep (ewes) will even take care of young rats and lambs they have never seen before with oxytocin injections.

During human labor, the uterine contractions of a mother cause the brain to produce an oxytocin flood and the dopamine neurotransmitter. The pain-removing effects of these hormones becomes necessary after a woman has worked 6 to 36 hours. When the baby is born and put to suckling, these hormones produce a trace of euphoria as a chemical flood high.

It is well understood that a mom who has decided to adopt her baby should not touch the infant since the touch and scent of the baby releases oxytocin. It can lead many mother to reconsider their decision to take the adoption path.

During the last month of pregnancy, the mother starts to manufacture the hormone for nutrition and lactation: prolactin. This hormone triggers her breasts to secrete milk. Oxytocin helps by allowing the liquid to be released from the breasts of a woman, and by sensitizing the new mother to the touch of her child. Yes, the brush of the baby's hand or lip on his mother's breast activates oxytocin. While breastfeeding, oxytocin increases, and the mother is happy and comfortable, and the mother-baby bond deepens.

When a man becomes a father, his brain chemistry changes too. Soon after listening to the news that he is about to be a dad, a man starts producing cortisol, a stress hormone. The amount of cortisol tends to increase four to six weeks after a man hears the news, and then decreases with the progression of the pregnancy. So, about three weeks before the kid arrives, his testosterone level falls by about 30%, making him more cooperative and less competitive.

In people, the hormone vasopressin plays a vital role in preparing a baby to be born and allowing men to make the new emotional connections of fatherhood.

CHAPTER 4
HOW INSECURE ATTACHMENT AFFECTS YOUR LOVE STYLE

Are you an insecure person? Are you shy? Do you fear the thought of being in front of people or speaking to someone special for fear of being rejected? The reality is that we all have felt this way many times during our lives. Fear of rejection and social anxiety is much more normal than we think. You can see it at school when peers don't want to come in front of the class to give a presentation. You can see it during the teenage years when your friends struggle to ask someone for a date, even asking the teacher a questions seems like something they want to avoid at all costs. But why? Where does insecurity come from?

There are many reasons why a person might be insecure. The environment where he was raised plays an important part. Perhaps this person was born in a family where social skills were never emphasized. Parents tend to put a lot of emphasis on academic achievement, which is not bad, but sometimes, they make the mistake of putting more emphasis on academic skills than social skills. The kid grows up believing that all he needs to do is study or comply with the house's rules to be completely happy. This idea is further emphasized when the kid is rewarded with presents that only fuel his desire to be in a bubble. After all, why would he have to go out if he has everything he needs to be entertained while at the same time being supervised by his parents?

Overprotection seems to go hand in hand with what has been described. Again, it's not bad at all to protect the people you love, but can a person realistically shield someone from all harm? The outcome is going to be the same in any case. What do you think will happen when the kid finally grows up and has to face the world? Do you think he will be prepared to tackle life's problems? Or do you think he will shudder at the first problem? Do you think he will continue trying after failing? Don't you think it's more reasonable to believe that he has gotten used to his parents' help so much that he might crave someone's help? It will be so easy for him to be attached to someone who helps him navigate life. Wasn't that the way his family raised him? He was always being watched and his goal was always to make someone else happy so it's only natural for him to find a significant other who makes him feel like he's "home" again.

Another reason for insecurity is the fact that people are taught by society that it's wrong for them to speak out because no one will care what they say or because of fear of being criticized or even harmed. They grow up in an environment of fear and isolation, which is the perfect breeding ground for anxiety. Ongoing ridicule is also a factor. Teased due to their physical or cultural differences, these people grow up with the idea that they are somehow inferior and nothing they say can be really taken seriously.

In the context of a relationship, people can become insecure if they have recently faced rejection or even unfaithfulness. They convince themselves they don't have any value in others' eyes, an idea that's very damaging to one's self-esteem. They ask themselves how this could ever have happened to them when everything seemed to be right. But here there's another underlying issue: perfectionism. Perfectionist people want their friendships, academic goals, and relationships, to live up to their own unreasonable standards. They think that by doing so they will achieve a greater goal and be happier, but in reality, they are setting themselves up for failure and heartbreak.

When expectations aren't realized in a relationship, one can suffer tremendously. "I thought we were perfect, why this is happening to me?" is one phrase that has been voiced by people with high and unrealistic expectations. Thinking that love and companionship will solve all their problems is a beautiful idea, but it's an unrealistic one. These people will end up disappointed and might easily give up when the relationship encounters difficult problems. Not being able to find the relationship they have always dreamt of makes them wonder if they can ever be loved, and so the insecurity of finding someone they can share life's moments takes hold of them.

How Insecurity Undermines a Relationship

A relationship is the union of two people who willingly accept each other's failings and learn how to put up with one another's differences. To some, this definition of a relationship might sound too cheesy, but there's much that can be found in this saying.

Accepting each other's failings means you understand the other person is as imperfect as you are and so he's bound to make many mistakes. There might be times when his words might hurt you and you might rightfully feel indignant or angry. But what about accepting your own failures? Is it easy for you to be modest and admit to your own mistakes?

Differences in upbringing might also show that both you and your partner have different communication styles: he might be someone who prefers discussing an argument after the water has calmed down, while you may be someone who wants to address any issue that seems to threaten the relationship. Therefore, finding a balance is key when dealing with problems in a relationship, whether they are considered "minor" problems or "serious" ones.

Insecurity lends itself to the doubts and uncertainties you see in the relationship. He is not in the mood for talking much lately. "Must be something I did," is what you tell yourself. But what if he has told you already that it's because he feels very stressed out and he needs some time for himself to feel recharged? Will you happily admit that he also needs time to relax or will you continue guessing why he doesn't feel like talking to you?

Do you like second guessing your partner's intentions, no matter how good they seem to be? Do you think he's always trying to hide something from you? Do you think he doesn't trust you anymore? It's easy to let yourself be consumed in these ideas; after all, there are many things that you just don't know about his day, and you don't know what he's thinking. But what all of these questions do is foster more insecurity in you. If you let yourself fall into the trap that the answers to these questions are worth scrutiny on your part, then you will be undermining one of the basis of any healthy relationship: trust.

If you've only dealt with the type of person that's always open to you and tells you everything, how will you be able to deal with a partner that's not secretive, but prefers to keep some things to himself?

Some measure of privacy and respect will always be appreciated in all relationships. Your partner will be grateful to you for showing respect and you'll be able to see that you also need some time for yourself to grow and develop as a person. Relationships outside the couple also need to be maintained to create a healthy environment where both know they are respected and interested in one another.

In the worst-case scenario, a relationship can even be destroyed if one makes a pest of himself by always checking the other's relationships and by thinking that there cannot be any uncertainties in their relationship. It's all too common to see how a relationship is brought to an end just because someone doesn't trust his partner and doesn't respect his right to make his own choices.

You don't need to become the one who will destroy the relationship. Avoiding that is possible if you learn how to manage the behaviors that lead to more insecurity and jealousy.

One manifestation of insecurity is being overly attached. There's nothing wrong with wanting to spend some time with our partner; actually, feeling connected to someone and demonstrating it is vital if you want to have a healthy and loving relationship. But this becomes a problem when it's taken to an extreme. Being overly attached poses a danger to your relationship and you need to learn how to manage it.

You're in no better position if you feel you're the one commanding. In a relationship, both will suffer. The one commanding and examining every movement is just showing how insecure he or she feels. The truth of the matter is that the relationship is not healthy. Just as an unreasonable boss is never satisfied with the explanations of his employee, the one demanding constant explanation from his partner will never be quiet, rather, he'll be finding excuses not to believe any explanation.

A mother might think that she's shielding her son by keeping him in a "bubble" where he is safe from threats, temptation, and danger. But the son will have to grow and mature. He will have to understand that life is also enjoyable outside the "bubble" where he was raised. By being overly attached to your partner, you might think you're protecting him from temptation or danger, but you're just stifling his enjoyment of life. You're just making him wonder what it feels like to be outside of your relationship. In other words, by being overly attached, you're giving him more reasons to end the relationship.

A prisoner might reassure himself by thinking about the day when his release will come. Don't let your relationship be like a prison where your partner finds reassurance only when he thinks about the day when he leaves the relationship.

You may feel overwhelmed and worried about what is happening, but find it difficult to actually pay attention to what is happening. When this occurs, your partner may feel as though you are not present. When you are anxious in your relationship, you may find it difficult to express your true feelings. If you don't express what you truly feel or need, anxiety becomes more intense and your emotions may begin to run out of control if you keep bottling them up. This leads to you feel overwhelmed and defensive.

Intimate relationships are able to reflect the best and worst of us all. They are mirrors that can fuel our struggles or calm them. Anxiety is a poison that can steal the joy and connection between two people who belong together. Perhaps you have been with your partner for a long period of time, yet you constantly wrestle with the notion that your partner doesn't live up to your expectations and will not be able to fill up that void in your heart.

Maybe you also suspect that you are a part of the problem. Perhaps you are insecure in love; you feel terribly lonely and desire a companion and lover to accompany you through the adventure and journey of life. You constantly wonder if anyone would be truly there for you if you let down your guard and are yourself. Would you be able to find comfort, reassurance, and support from them in your vulnerability? You ponder these things at every opportunity.

CHAPTER 5
ATTACHMENT AND FRIENDSHIP

It should be evident just how deeply our attachment style can affect our romantic relationships, along with our relationships with our parents and/or children. But our attachment style can also have a significant impact on our friendships and wider social networks. This includes our interactions with friends in person, along with our behaviors on social media sites such as Facebook.

Friendship for Secure Attachment Personalities

People with a secure attachment style have a heightened emotional intelligence which allows them to communicate effectively with those around them. They are able to interpret both verbal and non-verbal cues, giving them strong empathetic skills. For this reason, people with secure attachment styles generally have no problem instigating and maintaining friendships. They make reliable friends and colleagues and flourish in group environments.

Friendship for Anxious Preoccupied Personalities

The anxious preoccupied's desperate need for attention and validation within romantic relationships also shows itself among friends.

People with an anxious preoccupied attachment style often feel as though they are giving far more to their friends than they are receiving.

As those of us with these tendencies can be very emotionally expressive, we like to show our friends just how much they mean to us – and can occasionally overdo it. Anxious preoccupieds often see themselves as less valuable than their friends and will behave accordingly. But for secures who don't view their friend as a "lesser person" than themselves, this anxious preoccupied behavior can be difficult to understand. As a result, anxious preoccupieds often have difficulty building close connections with their friends.

If you have this attachment style, you may find yourself drawn towards friends who also exhibit anxious preoccupied tendencies. This will result in a friendship in which you both go out of your way to ensure the other knows how much you mean to them. While this can work, it is often characterized by desperation and neediness, and does not lead to the healthiest of relationships.

People with this attachment style are unlikely to maintain friendships with avoidant types, as the anxious need for attention is likely to drive the other person away before the friendship has time to develop.

Friendship for Dismissive Avoidant Personalities

While the way dismissive avoidants relate to their friends is completely opposite to anxious preoccupied personalities, the result is the same: a lack of close friendships. As we have learned, dismissive avoidants prize themselves on their independence and their perceived belief that they do not need anyone else in order to prosper. This can cause them to be distant and dismissive – something their secure friends will perceive as coldness, disinterest or even rudeness.

Friendship for Fearful Avoidant Personalities

While we all have versions of ourselves that we put out into the public eye, fearful avoidant personalities are adept at presenting a carefully cultivated persona, or false self when showing themselves to the world. This façade is a defense mechanism to prevent any spontaneous display of emotion and to keep their innermost feelings hidden away.

People who consider themselves friends with a fearful avoidant personality can often find themselves surprised and hurt when distress causes the fearful avoidant's "mask" to fall away. Their friends will then discover that the true personality of the person they had believed themselves close to was little more than a lie.

As a result of this false self, the fearful avoidant often has a group of friends that has been attracted to his or her fake persona and has little idea who they really are. When their true self is revealed in times of crisis, they may find they have no one who truly understands them – or perhaps even likes them – and consequently, they have no one on whom they can really rely.

Not being able to be vulnerable with friends who are vulnerable with you puts a strain on the relationship, making close friendships a challenge for fearful avoidants. It is important for people with this attachment type to recognize that real intimacy and friendship are based on loyalty and honesty. Pretending to be something you are not – while it can be an effective defense mechanism – will leave you with few friends you can count on in times of trouble.

Tie Strength and Multiplexity

Researchers at Australia's Deakin University and the Middle East Technical University in Turkey have determined the role of attachment styles as related to our friendship groups and social networks.

Their study examined "tie strength" and "multiplexity" within their subjects' social networks.

"Tie strength" refers to how close the ties in your network are; in other words, how comfortable you feel going to your friends for love and support in times of emotional distress. It also takes into consideration how often subjects interact with those in their network.

"Multiplexity" refers to having many different roles fulfilled by the same members of a subject's network. For example, a person who is both a colleague and a fellow member of a sports team has a high level of multiplicity. Similarly, if a subject feels close enough to a work colleague to go to them for advice and support, it also shows a high level of multiplexity.

Within an Avoidant Style...

The study shows that people with avoidant attachment styles have a weaker tie strength to members of their social network. This makes sense, given the avoidant's tendencies to shy away from affection. Similarly, avoidant behavior also leads to lower multiplexity within friendships, meaning the bond an avoidant has with their friends and colleagues is weaker and less reliable. They are less likely to actively maintain ties and are more likely to actively dissolve their friendships.

Within an Anxious Attachment Style...

Those with an anxious preoccupied attachment style are also likely to see the frequent dissolution of friendship ties. However, in their case, it is likely to be instigated by their contacts, rather than by themselves. As we know, people with an anxious attachment style have a need for constant attention and validation. This behavior can be smothering, leading to their friends and contacts to step away and dissolve the friendship.

Size of Your Social Network

You may assume that the larger a person's friendship network – either on or offline – the more popular and secure they are. However, this is not always the case.

Think about the size of your own social network. If you have hundreds, or even thousands, of connections on sites such as Facebook, think about how often you connect with the majority of people in this network. In all likelihood, not very often. The sheer numbers involved usually make this far too difficult. Similarly, if you have a huge circle of friends in "real life," it can be difficult to maintain close and meaningful relationships with all of them.

Studies support this, proving that the larger the friendship network, the weaker the ties and multiplexity of those connections.

Does this mean we should cull our Facebook pages and cut down our number of friends? Not necessarily. But it is important to recognize social media connections can never take the place of real-life friendships. While it can be easier to cultivate friendships behind the safety of the computer screen, putting yourself out into the real world and facing the challenges thrown up by your attachment style is the only way to build valuable, long-lasting friendships.

What Makes a Good Friend?

Knowing what we look for in a friend can go a long way towards helping us build long-lasting friendships. It reduces the potential for conflict and drama and helps us manage any problems that may arise due to our attachment issues.

Firstly, take some time to determine what makes a good friend in your opinion. Perhaps they are those who:

Show genuine interest in you and your life

Are always there for you in times of need

Don't judge you, even when you make mistakes

Never deliberately hurt your feelings

Never put you down

You enjoy their company

Are loyal and trustworthy

You can laugh and cry with

Will tell you the truth, even when it is hard to hear

Will always listen

You feel comfortable sharing your emotions with

Ask yourself how you feel when you're around a particular person. Does spending time with them make you feel better or worse? Are you yourself when you're around this person, or do you put on a façade, uncomfortable with revealing your true self? Does this person treat you with respect? Do you feel as though this is a person you can trust? (Incidentally, these are all excellent questions to ask yourself when navigating early romantic relationships too.)

How to be a good friend

The best way of maintaining lasting friendships, of course, is to be a good friend yourself. Think back to the characteristics that you determined make a good friend, and ensure you are exhibiting these traits in your own relationships.

Here are just a few of the ways you can work towards being a good friend towards those you care about:

Listen: If a friend is sharing his or her problems with you, ensure you engage in active listening; concentrate, do your best to retain information and offer a well thought out response. Ask questions. Do your best to see the situation from your friend's point of view. If you don't have all the answers, don't worry. Likely, your friend is not coming to you for a solution to their problem, they just need a sympathetic ear on which to unload. This can be a particularly difficult thing to do if you suffer from an avoidant attachment style, which is characterized by a lack of empathy.

Ask what you can do to help: If your friend is facing a difficult situation, don't wait for them to ask for ask help. Instead, actively ask them what they need and what you can do to help. This will lead them to reciprocate when you find yourself in a challenging situation.

Show physical affection: This can be another big challenge for those with avoidant attachment styles. But hugging your friends is a great way to show you care, and the physical contact increases the bond between you. All humans need physical contact with others in order to survive. An act as simple as a hug can prevent both you and your friend from feeling alone.

Keep in touch: Keeping in touch with our friends can be difficult at times, especially for those of us with large friendship circles and social networks. But taking time out of your busy schedule to connect with a friend is a great way to maintain closeness and strength in the friendship. It doesn't need to be a long-winded phone call. If you are short on time, send a short text or message on social media, just to let your friend know you are thinking of them.

Share your feelings: Tell your friends what they mean to you. Just as in romantic relationships, your friends can't be expected to know how you feel if you have not told them. This is especially true for friends with anxious preoccupied personalities. This kind of honesty and openness goes a long way towards building lasting friendships. And for those of you who feel uncomfortable opening up and sharing your feelings, remember that the more you do it, the easier it will get.

CHAPTER 6
DATING AND INSECURE ATTACHMENT

Do you find yourself on an endless cycle of awkward first dates and relationships that fizzle out before they've even begun? Can you see the same patterns of behavior emerging in all your relationships – both your own behavior and that of your partner? Do you find yourself always dating the same kind of men or women? Or do you constantly find yourself sabotaging relationships the moment they show any kind of promise?

If your answer to any of these questions is yes, you've likely come to realize that your attachment style is to blame. Depending on our own tendencies, we are drawn to people who exhibit particular characteristics, which explains why we can constantly end up dating people with the same damaging traits and behaviors.

So, what are we to do? Sit at home in front of the TV every night? Resign ourselves to a life of being alone? Not at all. Even for those of us with an insecure attachment style, dating doesn't need to be a struggle. It all comes down to understanding ourselves and, wherever possible, our partners.

By now, you're familiar with the traits of each attachment style and the love styles they give rise to. So, when you're next with your partner, or on a date, use this information to determine the attachment style and corresponding traits, of your partner.

We will take a look at what you can expect when dating people with each love attachment style. We will then look at all the possible attachment style combinations and some of the challenges that each coupling may face – along with methods for managing conflict and working towards building a healthy, long-lasting relationship.

Anxiety is a real challenge as well as a mental health disorder, which can lead to a lot of other problems if not properly checked. However, everyone develops anxiety from time to time, and it only becomes an issue if it is severe.

Anxiety can impact your relationships negatively, especially if you spend a great deal of time worrying and thinking about everything that could go wrong or has already gone wrong with the relationship. Here are some questions that may run through your mind when you are too anxious in a relationship:

What if they don't love me as much as I love them?

What if they're lying to me?

What if they're cheating on me?

What if I'm not good enough in the future for them?

What if they find someone else more attractive?

What if their family doesn't love me?

What if they die?

What if they bail out on me?

It is normal to have some of these thoughts, especially in a new relationship. However, when thoughts like these come to your mind frequently, it might be a sign of anxiety issues or an anxiety disorder. The intensity with which you constantly ruminate over the questions listed above and other questions that are similar determines how severe your anxiety problem. It will also determine how insecure you are in your relationship.

These anxious thoughts are manifested in diverse physical ways and present as symptoms such as shortness of breath, insomnia, and anxiety or panic attacks. You may discover that whenever you think this way, you trigger a panic attack in which your heart may begin to beat fast, a hard lump forms in your chest, and you begin to shake all over your body. These are the physiological signs that you are suffering from an anxiety disorder.

In some cases, these anxious thoughts encourage your partner to behave in ways that further stress you out and strain the relationship. This is because you are transparent enough to your partner that they can see you are very insecure. This gives them a manipulative edge over you, to twist and turn events in ways that normally should not mean a thing but will eventually hurt you and confirm one or two of the anxious beliefs you have.

For example, say you are worried and anxious about being the first to initiate a conversation all the time. You become sick in your mind that your partner doesn't like you because they don't take the first step in communicating as often as you do. The anxiety builds up and gathers momentum, and you begin to believe they might never chat with you or call you up if you do not reach out first.

To address this anxiety, you decide it is a good idea to go mute on them for a while. This forces your partner to communicate with you, reaching out a few times until you feel reassured knowing they will make the effort. This evidence allows you to challenge your anxious, irrational belief that they will not reach out first. This, however, is not a healthy strategy. Dealing with the root cause of anxiety and regaining your confidence is the best way to overcome anxiety disorder and leave you with a free and joyful life.

Intimate relationships are emotionally intense. This is due to the closeness that you share with another person. Alas, that closeness can make you feel powerless at times and can lead to anxiety and insecurity. Anxiety is fear of the unknown, while insecurity is self-doubt and the absence of self-confidence. Most times, insecurity graduates into anxiety if not properly managed.

It is also important to note that when you worry constantly in your relationship, you develop low self-esteem and ultimately insecurity sets in. You begin to see your partner's intentions or actions in a negative light; you view your partner as intimidating or critical.

Some symptoms of intense anxiety disorder can include:

A feeling of restlessness

Tensed muscles

Difficulty concentrating or remembering

Procrastinating or having trouble making decisions

Worry that leads to repeatedly asking for reassurance

Inability to get enough sleep and rest

Inasmuch as relationships are very beautiful and pleasurable, they can also breed anxious thoughts and feelings. These thoughts can arise at any stage of the relationship. If you aren't in a relationship yet, the thought of meeting the right person and being in a relationship can already generate anxiety for you, which you must deal with.

Severe insecurity steals your peace and prevents you from engaging with your partner in a relaxed and authentic way. The actions arising from insecurity may include jealousy, false accusations, snooping, lack of trust, and seeking reassurance and validation. These attributes are not conducive to a healthy relationship and can push your partner away.

Most people believe that insecurity stems from the actions or inaction of their partners. The reality is that most insecurity comes from within you. You build insecurity when you negatively compare yourself to other people and judge yourself harshly with your inner critical voice. A lot of the insecurities in your relationship are based on irrational thoughts and fears that you are not good enough and that you are not capable of making someone else happy. But these aren't true!

When you start to notice that uneasy feeling of being insecure, one thing you can do is to begin taking stock of your value. Insecurity makes you focus on something you feel is lacking within you. In most balanced relationships, each partner brings different strengths and qualities that complement each other. In order to conquer your insecurity, take stock of the value you offer to your partner. Personality and a great character are important qualities to the overall health of a relationship.

Building your self-esteem is also crucial to surmounting any insecurity you face in your relationship. It is important that you feel good about who you are on the inside in order to not constantly seek validation from someone else. You are complete within yourself and you must let your independence and self-worth shine brightly through your deeds and actions. When your well-being depends on someone else, you give them the key to your joy and you empower them. This may be quite unhealthy for your partner to bear and certainly does not work well for a relationship. One way to build your self-confidence is to silence your inner critic and focus your mind and attention on positive qualities. Look in the mirror and speak positive affirmations to yourself – looking yourself in the eye when you do this makes a greater impact than simply telling yourself in your head that you're worthy of love.

You should also be able to maintain your sense of self-identity and be able to cater to your personal well-being. If before the relationship you were doing a great job of tending to your physical, mental, and emotional needs, this should not stop now just because you are in a relationship. You should maintain your independence and not allow yourself to turn into someone who is needy or attached. Being an independent person who has a life and identity outside of the relationship also makes you a more interesting and attractive partner. Your life must continue to move forward and make considerable progress when you are in a relationship. Being in a relationship is not the final phase of your life, and you should continue to be driven and achieve more goals, which can further endear you to your partner.

Some ways to maintain your independence include cultivating and nurturing great friendships, making time for your own friends, interests, and hobbies, maintaining financial independence, constantly improving yourself, and setting high standards for your dreams.

CHAPTER 7
HOW TO FIND YOUR PARTNER

You may have learned it from friends or co-workers a few times. They talk about how beautiful their relationship is. It's new, and they're excited. Some months later, they begin to say things like, "I'm just not sure he's the one for me." They can't put their finger on it, but for them, something doesn't work. You begin to think about your relationship. Is he the right person for you? How are you?

One of the most important issues when it comes to finding someone you like is the way they treat you. Are they kind, compassionate, caring, or respectful? Do they keep the conversation on the floor, or do they stand up? Such definitions are now quite straightforward. Here are some things to keep in mind when you start dating somebody to see if they fit you well:

Ensure that your relationship is consistent with your values. Most people conform to the ideals of the person they are dating. They don't know their principles, so they just try and fit what they're given. Take some time to consider your own beliefs. When you love fun and speak to someone who is severe, it won't match well most of the time.

Secondly, make sure you know what you want in a person. Sure, you want them to be attractive and kind, but what else in a human do you want? Is their job something that matches what you want? For instance, you meet a great person, you start dating, and things are going well. The only thing is that they always go to work. They are out of the city more often than in the city. Is that something with which you are comfortable? It is essential to know the answer. When you say "I'm OK, but it's not my dream," then you might need to explain your needs. You might end up raising your children with a partner who is gone quite often if you continue the relationship and end up married.

Thirdly, similar interests are significant. Now, this doesn't mean that you have to be joined the hip, but you should enjoy some joint activities. If you have too many different interests, one of you will end up sacrificing your happiness. Think about how much time you want your partner to invest. If you're going to be with somebody most of the time, you have to enjoy yourself, and vice versa.

Fourth, understand that not necessarily every person you meet is the person you will want to marry. Just because someone is sweet and seems perfect for you at first, if you later uncover things that do not match your standards, it's all right to let them go and move on. Understand that every person you meet gives you valuable information. It is essential to understand that each person you meet gives you a clearer picture of want and do not want.

But you must understand that you can't be too picky. The above step appears to be a contradiction, but it is indeed an add-on. Nobody, not even you, is perfect. You may have many qualities you want in a person, and your partner may have most, but not all of them. This is all right. Find those whose qualities are most important to you and keep them close to your heart.

All these steps help you to decide whether this partner is right for you. You deserve the best friendship, and there's someone for everyone if you're prepared to do the internal work you need to.

Building Healthy Relationships

Cupid's bow and arrow in hand is often used as a representation of magical love. What could be more romantic than some twist of fate bringing you together with your significant other for a happily-ever-after ending? You may be one of those hopeless romantics who believe in soulmates and "the one," or you may be a believer in making your own destiny.

It doesn't really matter which of the two notions you subscribe to because when it comes right down to it, all healthy relationships require effort and a willingness to create the reality you want. There is no harm in being romantic or believing that there is a soulmate for everyone. However, you must be willing to do the work to create your own happily-ever-after. The honeymoon phase does not last forever, and after it has passed, you will need a lot more than romance to keep your relationship healthy.

Healthy and happy relationships are built on commitment, finding freedom in that commitment and awareness. Most people think of commitment as the ball and chain that signals an end to their freedom. Actually, this assumption is quite far off the mark. In a healthy relationship, commitment signals freedom. Freedom to be yourself, freedom to be vulnerable, and the freedom to give in to your innermost desires.

If your relationship feels like a ball and chain, then you need to rethink the kind of reality you have created for yourself. Being in a relationship should make you feel like you have found the person you want to share your life with. This should free you from the anxiety of constantly dating or trying to find someone you can connect with. Unfortunately for most people, this reality is forgotten when they get into a relationship.

Ironically, when it comes to relationships, those who are in them are trying to get out and those who are outside are trying to get in. This is especially common when you find yourself in a relationship where you feel trapped or like you are no longer free to be yourself. Fortunately, creating a healthy relationship is a skill that can be learned. No matter how many failed relationships you have had, there is nothing standing in the way of you having a successful relationship.

Any relationship that is worth having can be fixed if the two parties in it are willing to do the work. The awareness part of being in a healthy relationship requires that no matter what is going on in your relationship, you always try to remember why you got together in the first place.

You can get so caught up in the troubles you are experiencing that you forget that the person you are fighting with, was once the person you considered "the one." Remember why you fell in love in the first place and resolve to work through your issues. Sometimes it is better to rebuild what you have than to keep jumping from one relationship to another hoping that the next one will be better.

Open Communication

If you want a healthy relationship, communication has to be one of the first things that you get right. By definition, communication is the transfer of information that lets the other person know what you are thinking or feeling. In a relationship, communication goes beyond just the words that are coming from your mouth. It defines how you connect with your partner and how you understand each other.

If you are with someone and you have no idea what they need or how they are feeling, how would it possible for that relationship to work? Communication affects all aspects of your relationship including intimacy. The more you are aware of each other's needs the better you will be at fulfilling them.

Overcoming Jealousy

The green-eyed monster can destroy even the strongest of relationships. It breaks down trust and creates tension in the relationship. One partner takes on an offensive role while the other becomes defensive. In this kind of dynamic, both parties are miserable, and the relationship begins to feel like a burden.

Jealousy is in most cases driven more by your insecurities than by your partner's actions or behavior. It can lead to people making rash decisions that end up causing more harm to the relationship. Lashing out, avenging and even aggression are just some of the ways in which jealousy manifests.

At some point or other we all experience jealousy. Sometimes it is founded while in others it can be a result of an overactive imagination and fear. Whatever the case may be, jealousy becomes a problem when you start giving in to it. Learning to manage your emotions is one of the most effective ways of overcoming jealousy and its effects on your relationship.

Emotional Connection Done Right

How do you avoid codependency and ensure your attachment style is positive? When you are in a relationship it is possible to get too attached and forget yourself. This happens when you make the other person the center of your universe and neglect your own needs. This kind of overdependency damages any chance of having a healthy relationship.

On the other hand, you do not want to be emotionally unavailable. People who are afraid of deep emotional connections tend to be closed off and detached. This again makes it impossible to have a healthy relationship. The trick to healthy emotional connection is finding the fine line between becoming overly dependent and being emotionally detached. This can only happen if you cultivate healthy independence while still maintaining an emotional connection to your partner.

Trust-Building Tips

Never make promises you cannot keep. No matter how much you want to please your partner, avoid making promises that you cannot keep. When you break them, their trust in you will start to waver.

Do what you say when you say. No matter how little or petty it seems, honor your commitments. Call when you say you will, show up when you promised to, and always stick to your word. No one likes a flaky person and trusting one is almost impossible.

Stop being a people pleaser. Be clear on where you stand on things so that your partner knows what you are feeling and thinking. Learn to say no when you cannot honor a commitment, it is better than saying yes then failing to do it.

Honesty is the best policy. Be truthful, nothing undermines trust faster than lies. Be upfront with your partner and tell them the truth, no matter how difficult it is.

Own up to your mistakes. When you are constantly blame-shifting and scapegoating, it becomes difficult for anyone to trust you. When you have the courage to own up to your mistakes, it tells people that you are not just honest with them but that you are also honest with yourself.

Be consistent. Do not be so unpredictable that your partner has no idea what you would do in any given situation. People trust you more when you are consistent in your behavior and actions. It shows them that you have certain values that you operate within.

CHAPTER 8
HOW TO FEEL GOOD WITHOUT A RELATIONSHIP

Everyone's story is different. You may be someone who needs just one wake up call to spur them into action or your detangling process may be more gradual.

Once you come to the realization that you are co-dependent, then your battle is halfway won. In the larger scheme of things, it is not the scars from your past that define you, rather it is the lessons you choose to take away from those scars. Do not be ashamed of your past, wear your experiences with pride and as a sign of just how far you have come.

No journey is ever completely smooth and there are a few universal truths that will help to keep you going. These truths are the tools you need to carry to remind you of just where you are going, what you have freed yourself from and most importantly, what you need to keep going.

The trick to real and lasting change is to do it in small and manageable doses. Do not overwhelm yourself with long lists of things you need to do or not do. Pick your struggles one at a time and take them apart one by one.

Self-Assertion

If you are a play-along-to-get-along kind of person then you probably do not like conflict. People who shy away from conflict or having to differ with others prefer to just accept other people's opinions even when they do not agree with them. This is especially true for co-dependents who are natural people pleasers.

If you have a problem with self-assertion you will often find yourself feeling resentful and angry and not have a clue why that is happening. When you constantly suppress your needs in order to accommodate and please other people, sooner or later the frustration of not having your needs met will start to show.

This frustration will manifest itself in the form of emotional outbursts over petty issues, moodiness, and feelings of resentment toward your partner. None of these feelings are recipes for a good relationship so it turns out that play-along-to-get-along does not really work in the long term.

The first thing you need to understand is that there is a world of difference between compromising and ignoring your needs. In a compromise, you and your partner acknowledge each other's needs and agree to meet halfway. Compromise is a healthy part of any relationship. However, when you ignore your needs it means you have not made the other party aware of your needs and you simply choose to focus on their needs. This is the classic trait of many co-dependents who feel the need to accommodate and people please.

Self-assertion is being able to clearly articulate your needs and let the other person know how you feel. Being assertive is part of open communication in a relationship. It lets your partner know what you expect from them and also what they can expect from you. This kind of communication is crucial in building better relationships.

You cannot blame your partner for not meeting your needs when you have not even communicated to them what those needs are. This means that as you recover from co-dependence, self-assertion is one of the skills you need to develop.

The benefits of being assertive:

It helps you to get things done

It earns you respect from the other party

It makes compromise and conflict resolution easy

It makes you less prone to anxiety and stress

Being assertive is not just better for your relationships, but it also makes you more confident.

Being Your Own Best Friend

Recovering from co-dependency is only possible if you are able to establish healthy self-esteem and a sense of self-worth. A person with a low sense of self-worth will naturally seek to get their validation from the other people in their lives.

This is what fosters co-dependency habits such as enabling, caretaking and many more. If you are to escape the trap of co-dependency, the first place you need to look is inward. Healthy self-esteem will solve most of the insecurities and fears that led to the development of co-dependency in the first place.

Fears like the fear of rejection and the fear of abandonment are all stoked by low self-esteem. To fight these fears, you need to cultivate a sense of safety and security that is tied to your own self-worth and not to other people. This will free you from the need to seek validation and approval from others.

When it comes to building self-esteem, this is pretty much an inside job that depends on your ability to change your opinion of yourself. This change is only possible if you learn to practice self-empathy and become your own best cheerleader.

Consider how you treat your friends. You compliment them, buy them gifts on their birthday, support them when they need you and help them celebrate their victories. You defend them from other people and feel protective over them. This is completely natural and healthy for a good relationship.

Here are some simple tips that will help you practice self-love and being your own best friend:

Spend time doing the things you love

Make time for your passions and the things that make you truly happy. Do not feel guilty about wanting some time to yourself to do something you love.

Get rid of negative energy

Free yourself from people who are always dragging you down and stealing your joy. Be selective about who you allow into your inner circle and life. Be ruthless when it comes to safeguarding your inner peace.

Focus on the positives

Don't be your own biggest critic. Focus on the things you love about yourself and accept your flaws as just a normal part of human nature.

No one is perfect and constantly focusing on your weaknesses will only undermine your confidence.

Take care of your body

Stay healthy and active. A healthy body builds your confidence and self-esteem. Take time to exercise and eat well. You only get one body in this life so take care of it. Avoid over-indulging in unhealthy habits that damage your health in the long run.

Stay true to your values

Keep your values close at heart and make decisions that are in line with your core values. Your values will help you make better choices and to avoid following trends and other people's opinions just to please others.

Saying No to Toxic Relationships

Perhaps one of the more challenging aspects of co-dependent tendencies is the propensity to soak up other people's distress. When you do not have sufficient boundaries to safeguard your emotions, you end up making other people's problems your own. This effectively leads you to a co-dependent situation where you are unable to separate yourself from the other person.

Such toxic relationships bring out the worst in you because the other person knows exactly what buttons to push to get you to toe the line. You will find yourself often doing things you would otherwise never consider doing just to keep the other person happy. This dysfunction, if left unchecked, becomes a self-repeating cycle that takes over your life.

Toxic relationships poison you from the inside out. In extreme cases, they may even drive you to coping mechanisms such as addictions to help you process your unresolved issues. This potential for self-harm is one of the reasons why freeing yourself from codependency requires that you eliminate any toxic relationships from your life.

Whether you are dealing with a narcissist who thrives on attention and being the center of the universe, or with more covert manipulators, the damage to your self-esteem is hard to repair. Toxic people come in many different shapes and forms and you need to be able to identify them by their characteristics.

Here are some of the warnings signs that you need to be on the lookout for if you are to identify toxic people and weed them out:

They like to control you

They like to shift blame and never take responsibility for their actions

They are overly critical and always trying to find fault

They use threats and intimidation to manipulate you.

They try to gain sympathy by playing with your emotions

They are always complaining

They often use emotional abuse to make you feel worthless

Perhaps the most toxic relationship for a co-dependent is one with a narcissist. Narcissists have no consideration or interest in other people's feelings or needs. When it comes to empathy and compassion, the narcissist is the polar opposite of the co-dependent.

Here are the classic signs that point to a narcissistic personality:

They lack empathy and never try to meet your needs

They manipulate you to get what they want

They expect you to cater to their every need and whim without question

They demand to have the best of everything

They are constantly making you feel inferior

They have a compulsive need to be the center of attention.

Knowing Which Walls to Build

When you think of walls, you immediately think of protection and safeguarding something. That is exactly what walls do in your emotional life as well. They keep the good stuff in and safeguard you from the negative. That is why you need to build walls around the things you need to keep protected.

Your values, your self-esteem, your interests, and your goals are some of the things that you need to protect at all costs. When you are in a co-dependent state, these pieces of you get lost in the relationship as you put all your energy into meeting the needs of the other person. In this case, you get lost in the relationship and lack any sense of self-worth or individuality.

To avoid falling into this trap, walls help you to create boundaries that set limits for yourself and the people in your life. These walls say to yourself and the people in your life that these are things I will not compromise on. Retaining your values, passions and interests is important in the journey of recovery from co-dependency.

Tips for Building Better Boundaries

Identify your limits

Identify what you want to protect and where essentially your limits are. Decide what you are willing to compromise on and what a deal-breaker is for you. You can base these decisions on your values and the things that are important to you.

Be assertive

Communicate your boundaries clearly and let the other person know what you expect from them and what they can expect from you. That way both parties are fully aware of what they are getting into and are fully prepared for it.

Cultivate self-awareness

The only way to set good boundaries is to understand yourself first. When you appreciate what your needs are, you can set reasonable boundaries that will help you meet your needs.

Consider your unresolved issues

Only you can know where your triggers and weaknesses are. Set boundaries that will help you cope with these weaknesses and make it easy for you to escape the traps that made you co-dependent in the first place.

Prioritize your needs

Boundaries should be about ensuring that whatever relationship you are getting into, your needs are being met. This means that your primary consideration when setting limits should be your needs and what you want from the relationship.

CHAPTER 9
DEALING WITH INSECURE ATTACHMENT ISSUES

Insecurities come from the past. Each time your insecurity is triggered, you are reliving past events that are holding you back. It's time to move forward and make peace with the past in order to live a happy, fulfilled life with your loved one. The path to achieving a healthy relationship is not an easy one, and it will take time, effort and persistence. Understanding all the aspects of your insecurity is an important part of moving forward. Without understanding, you wouldn't be able to make the first steps and invest effort in getting better. Bringing your insecurities to your awareness will already do wonders, if in nothing else, then in motivating you to fight them. Insecurities manifest themselves as subconscious fears, parts of our defensive mechanisms, tricks and traps of our mind that are holding us back. It is hard to be actively aware, especially in stressful situations and in those first moments when insecurity is triggered. But now you can be aware that it is your inner critical voice speaking; it is not the real you. It's a distorted perception of yourself that is playing with your emotions, using your insecurities to deepen the fear and protect you from being hurt. These defensive mechanisms were useful when we were infants and children. They got stuck with us in adulthood, but now they are doing more harm than help, and it's time to overcome them.

Learn to Accept

What you've been doing wrong thus far is that you are putting your effort into controlling your core belief. While doing so, you created new pains that pushed you into behaviors that are harming your relationship. You might have isolated yourself, felt uncontrollable anger, or tried to control others. Your efforts to control the uncontrollable pain are hurting you more and more. It's time to consider changing your tactic. Instead of fighting, it is much healthier to allow yourself to feel all the negative emotions that come when your core belief is triggered. It is time to stop fighting and accept defeat in order to be able to transform. It is hard to accept the defeat, and even harder to understand that you need to feel the pain. But if you do this, you will also feel relieved because you won't have to put in all the emotional effort needed when battling an enemy you can't defeat. All the useless struggles you went through trying to control your core belief will go away. The pain will remain, but now you don't have to fight it, you can listen to it and you might learn something from it.

Live By Your Values

As we all have imprinted core beliefs and insecurities, we also have imprinted values; characteristics we find useful and that make us happy. These are imprinted on us by our parents, society, and the culture we live in. They are based on morals, personality, and by the society we grew up in. Values vary in different parts of the world, and they can seem pretty personal. It is important to recognize the values you have so you can consciously decide to live by them. Here is a short list of values: Duty, fun, commitment, confidence, affection, clarity, enthusiasm, honor, courage, family, creativity, imagination, freedom, pleasure, loyalty, teamwork, truth, virtue, openness, security, sexuality, wisdom, peace.

Emotional intelligence is much more than a set of approaches and strategies that serve to better identify and manage our own emotions. Above all, we are talking about gaining a true emotional awareness with which to build stronger, more respectful relationships, and being a power key with which we feel safer, more successful, and happier.

Long before Daniel Goleman published his famous book *Emotional Intelligence* in 1995, this term had already appeared in the scientific world at the hands of Michael Beldoch in 1964 and in several articles. These articles spoke of communication and emotional sensitivity, their implications, and how they determine our relationships and personality. Since then, the theme has advanced remarkably, giving rise to different approaches and criticisms.

There are many experts who do not see scientific rigor in the subject, who do not accept the idea that emotional intelligence is "another" type of intelligence, but rather a domain of it, a skill. However, the implication that this psychological, social and motivational perspective has on our daily lives goes beyond the possible gaps that may or may not exist in Goleman's theory.

Emotional intelligence improves our quality of life, interpersonal relationships, our own perception, and even our professional competence. In addition, it is an approach that should inform most school curricula to educate more competent, safe and happy people.

Applying this emotional awareness is key to improving our own personal and social reality. Let's see why.

Emotional Intelligence, the Key to a More Fulfilling Life

From childhood, many of us were guided along the path of emotional restraint. Almost unknowingly, our parents and educators advised us not to cry, "You are already a big child," "If you are angry, hang on," or that common phrase, "You take everything very seriously."

This scarce sensitivity to one's own or others' emotional world still determines many scenarios that we go through in our daily lives. In the family context, this tendency to camouflage emotions is still very present, not to mention in our workplaces, where the hierarchical organizations led by leaders continues to triumph, aiming to achieve immediate goals and creating an oppressive and stressful professional climate.

Goleman points out that emotional intelligence is present in any relationship, and that, in turn, has a fundamental goal: to offer us a life of more fulfillment.

Reasons Why Emotionally Smart People Are Happier

Think for a moment of emotional intelligence as an antenna. An antenna with double pickup: indoor and outdoor. Thanks to it we learn to know each other better, to understand the ball of our emotions and, in turn, to understand that of others.

Thanks to emotional intelligence we are more aware of ourselves.

We deal better with our own emotional universes.

We develop greater emotional and cognitive empathy.

We are more committed to ourselves.

We build greater social awareness.

Emotional Intelligence Skills in the Workplace

The work paradigm is changing. The very real possibility of more automated work or tasks being performed by machines or robots has led experts in this area to alert us of something very feasible: in the future technical knowledge will not be valued, but personal skills will be prioritized.

Therefore, skills such as creativity, critical thinking, ingenuity, and emotional intelligence are key to a more automated professional world.

Emotional Intelligence as "Fuel" in Children's Education

Emotional intelligence is a key power to develop in children to enhance their ability to build more positive relationships with their families and peers, to develop a more balanced view of life, and to achieve good academic potential in school. In the end, being able to manage and understand one's emotional world means having an exceptional channel for learning, attention, memory, and to control frustration.

Reasons Why Emotionally Focused Therapy Works So Effectively to Restore the Love and Connection in Your Relationship

EFT is based on extensive research

Emotionally Focused Therapy (EFT) is a pair therapy research-based approach founded by Drs. Susan and Les Greenberg Johnson. It is based on attachment theory and extensive research in neuroscience about the innate need of humans to feel attached and comforted by their significant others. The techniques used in EFT to mend and improve relationships between couples and families are built through ongoing research on approaches and processes that most effectively restore faith in relationships and reinforce the intrinsic bond of connection at the heart of all successful relationships of love.

EFT addresses universal attachment needs

We now realize that the need for attachment is universal and works at all ages. Indeed, recent research shows that relationships of adult attachment have the same function of survival as the parent-child bond – providing a safe person to contact for comfort and reassurance in order to meet the challenges of life and take risks necessary for personal growth.

EFT gets right to the heart of the conflict

Conflict and disconnection between partners are the number one reason people seek advice. Conflicts over jealousy, sex, finance, parenting, in-laws or other issues are not just about the specific content about which you argue. Such challenges are about your partner not being noticed, understood and respected at their heart.

There is no question that the latest neuroscientific research indicates that we all need our partners to be open, sensitive and emotionally engaged with us. When the most important person in our life is not present, or our need to feel near and protected is not met, we feel distressed and often get angry, anxious, afraid, distant or numb. Regardless of the content, the underlying truth is that we all need assurance that we are cared for and that when we need them, our partner will be there for us.

EFT heals what matters

We all need to ask in our close relationships, "WHEN I NEED YOU, WILL YOU BE THERE FOR ME?" EFT was designed to help you fix the deep hurts, disrespect, and losses that couples experience. Pleas for affection, acceptance, encouragement, security and comfort are just under harsh words and angry voices. Over time, you will start hearing and understanding each other with encouragement and respond effectively to each other in a safe and loving manner.

EFT builds security

The primary task of Emotionally Focused Therapy is to help you and your partner become the safe haven and stable foundation for each other. It will help you understand and improve the way you and your partner interact, feel close to each other, and experience each other in a more loving way. The effect is a more constructive pattern that fosters affection, confidence, and attachment as you change your negative patterns of communication.

EFT fosters effective communication.

After alteration of the destructive pattern, each of you will start to calm down and feel comfortable with the other. Without so much of the past defensiveness, each of you will be better able to send clear messages to each other, speak from the heart, consider the viewpoint of each other, and really solve the conflict.

EFT produces results that last

Even after the completion of counseling, research shows that most people are more capable of communicating with effectiveness and affection. Also, you will be better able to work together, solve problems, and repair relationship conflicts when they occur. You will build a true partnership and appreciate the continuing friendship, warmth, passion, and love of a relationship that is firmly attached to you.

CHAPTER 10

THE NEW SKILLS YOU NEED TO LEARN

Communication skills in a love relationship

In the face of problems that may arise from conflicts in a love relationship, a good communicative ability is perhaps the best antidote for reaching a joint and agreed solution. And the best ingredients for cooking up this solution are respect, understanding, and kindness.

Besides, it is essential to learn to communicate appropriately, as we sometimes say things out of time or at the least convenient time. This sometimes makes our treatment of the other person inappropriate.

Problems arise when we try to guess the other person's thoughts or feelings, as we often make mistakes in the conclusions we draw. We also tend to generalize – "You always do the same thing," "Never listen to me," "You're a grandpa," rather than specifying what we like or don't in a clear manner. Not only that, it is important that our nonverbal conduct coincides with what we are talking about and is not contradictory.

So what aspects can we improve when we communicate in a love relationship?

Regarding this nonverbal conduct, some aspects need to be considered. Firstly, in interpersonal communication, it is important to maintain eye contact, as well as to adapt facial expressions to the situation and ensure they are in line with the message we want to transmit. It is good if our body posture represents attention toward the other person. And finally, it is recommended that both the volume and tone of voice be quiet and smooth.

Be spontaneous, smile and don't be afraid to laugh at what you find funny. Have freedom with your love. Don't get caught up in the doubts and uncertainties that surround your mind. Be yourself in any situation without being ashamed of the wonderful person you are.

Don't expect to suffer, don't create monsters in your head, don't choose to live under fear. If he doesn't call, wait the next day without anxiety. Living in a relationship and expecting to suffer is long-term suicide. Let freedom strengthen this relationship.

Don't make up fights for anything. Think carefully about whether this or that is worth fighting for. Ponder and always, always, analyze before you explode. When you fail and feel you have hit the ball, apologize. It's beautiful to apologize.

Put yourself in the other's shoes. Imagine if it were with you in the situation; how would you react? What words would you use to explain yourself? How would you handle all this? Once you have this insight, you are ready to resolve this conflict.

Don't fill up with messages, but send a message from time to time, saying 'I miss you.' Tell your loved one you wish he or she were here right now to see your face swollen from the dentist's anesthesia. Finally, connect with your love and your partner's love.

Surprises and mysteries are great aphrodisiacs; they keep that flame alive that makes a life for two so delicious. So, create moments. Schedule a surprise trip. Make a romantic dinner. Buy a gift and provide clues for a treasure hunt.

Cultivate habits together, whether it's taking a walk or watching a movie over the weekend. This will create harmony and bring complicity. It will be your moment, and nobody comes in, nobody leaves.

Don't take everything so seriously, laugh at life together. Did that quarrel last Saturday continue to this day? Raise the white flag with a lot of humor.

Be more tolerant of each other's mistakes. We are all human beings, and everyone is wrong sometimes. Don't want to put an end to the relationship because of every small blunder. Evaluate the conditions and see what really suits you; if it really is unbearable, then it is better that the relationship comes to an end, but if it is silly mistakes, forgive.

Don't cancel yourself out for your love. Have your privacy, your date with friends, your time to be alone. Even though you are in the same boat, you and your partner have independent lives and that life must remain unique for the union to strengthen. No one can stand to be in a rut from anyone for a long time, because we all have problems, sadness; everyone has a life. Do not invent crutches, walk with your own legs.

Practice unconditional acceptance

Occasionally, we secretly want the other person to change to suit our wishes or standards. That is, we somehow want things to be different than they are. The problem is that this attitude can lead us to feel a lot of frustration, since the other will not always act as we expect, in fact, if he did, he would stop being himself.

Learning to love the other as they are, accepting their way of being, is essential if we want to maintain a relationship. Of course, this does not mean we have to accept disrespectful behaviors or generate suffering. There are impassable limits.

Now, it is important that we keep in mind that the other person is acting in the best way he knows based on his experience – except for toxic and abusive relationships. As a rule, most of us do not act with bad intentions. Therefore, it is best to try to understand and talk about what we feel uncomfortable with.

Having this in mind helps to nurture an attitude of kindness towards the other, even in the most complicated moments.

Learn to be with yourself

When the indifference towards being in a couple has ended the relationship, many wonder: what now? Some people are inclined to look for another person, that is, they feel the need to fill that void by initiating another relationship. Others prefer to be alone for a while. However, when a relationship ends, the best option is to learn – to learn to be with ourselves. In this way, we will avoid falling into another relationship through dependence.

There are a large number of people unable to lead a life without someone by their side. However romantic this may seem, what lies behind this generated need is a high factor of emotional dependence.

Many are terrified of being with themselves, having no one to hug, listening to their thoughts or identifying what they want and don't want. There is an inner emptiness that they intend to fill with external affection. In this way it is very difficult to wait for a person who really fits, thus condemning the new relationship to a premature end.

Learn to be alone

Life is prettier with love, but it is more healthy when we feel good about ourselves. Therefore, to eliminate emotional dependence, it is necessary to learn to be alone. Enjoy and understand yourself. Delve into who you are, what you want and whatnot.

When one loves oneself and does not need others, one is then prepared to love in a healthy way.

We would all like to have an ideal partner, people to love. But need and desire are very different things. When we need it doesn't work. When we have to have someone by our side to feel good, it is very likely that the relationship will not develop in a healthy way.

One must learn to enjoy life without a partner. There are countless things to do, such as discovering and developing our skills, carving out our future, dedicating time to hobbies, making friends with good people, traveling, enjoying little things. And above all take care of and love yourself as you deserve.

Learn to deactivate the ego

We need to understand that the ego is a way of "disconnecting" completely from the axes that move conscious love, the mature love that is offered in freedom and fullness to another to form a couple, to have a common project of always respecting the personal growth of each other.

If your partner is a skilled artisan of "selfishness," set limits from the beginning and make it very clear that love is not about judging, controlling, or even filling in the gaps and insecurities of your own through manipulation. To love is not to offer burdens, but inner growth. Fullness.

We need to begin to enunciate to do things as our ego wants and enjoy them as they happen. It is then that our true awareness of love will wake up; that which stops fighting to give way to the spontaneity of everyday life, to freedom where there are no attachments and where each person is the owner of himself, and in turn, part of a common project.

Is it possible to change the attachment pattern we learned in childhood?

We could define attachment as a bond created between two people that makes them want to stay together in space and time. This union is created in the first months of life with the primary caregiver and governs the kind of relationships that will guide us in future. However, is it possible to change the attachment pattern set in childhood?

Psychoanalyst John Bowlby devoted himself to the study of attachment and established that the process begins shortly after birth, but it is not until about eight months that the first attachment bond between the baby and the primary caregiver can be considered.

Unsafe preventive attachment: By this point, the baby has learned that the power he has to produce reactions in the people around him is very limited. Thus, the most common reaction to this is that he is not very expressive.

Insecure-ambivalent-resistant attachment: The child has had crying episodes in which he has been comforted and others in which he has not received the same attention. This creates uncertainty in facing the world. She feels she has the power to produce an effect on others, but she also "understands" that effect is unpredictable.

Our attachment style makes us create a first image of what surrounds us, what we internalize very deeply. Unless we can learn other patterns later, we understand that this is the way we relate to the people we love.

CHAPTER 11
CHANGE YOUR BEHAVIOR

The success of a relationship is dependent upon the willingness of the partners to equally put in effort. When it's only one person that seems to get it right, it cannot work, because they eventually become frustrated.

Being in a relationship with someone that struggles with insecure attachment issues can be problematic because they have a poor attitude and suspicion, and these two factors are unforgiving agents of ruin.

You can't change your emotions that are products of your insecurities, but you can change the way you respond to those emotions and core beliefs. There are two things you need to do so you can change your behavior successfully: be aware of your current behavior and how it influences your relationship and then do the opposite.

Become Aware of your Behavior

Our behaviors that come from insecurities are nothing more than patterns that we must break in order to change the influence of insecurity on our relationship. If you look back on your past behaviors, you will have the best possible chance to change them in future. Don't be ashamed of your past behaviors, and don't think of them as something bad. They were unhelpful, for sure, and that is the only term we need to be aware of. Now we want to change our behaviors to helpful.

Think back to what situations trigger your insecurities. Do you have a response to those situations that repeat themselves? Maybe it is a combination of responses. If you have abandonment insecurities, are you prone to withdraw from your partner but suddenly become clingy and dependent? Do you notice such a pattern in your behavior? Feel free to write down your insecurities, what triggers them and how you behave in response to them. Notice the pattern and become aware of it. Don't judge your past behaviors; true they might not be pleasant, but behaviors are coping mechanisms designed to deal with emotional pain. They didn't work, but they were the only mechanisms you had. Now you will learn new ones – helpful ones, and you will see your relationship become more enjoyable for both you and your partner.

To better understand your past behaviors, try to remember how your partner responded to them. Think how your partner behaved immediately after your insecurity was triggered and what his long-term response was. Did he get angry? Was he sad? Did he stop calling you? The insecurities are making you behave negatively, and your partner has no other choice than to respond negatively. This is due to something that's popularly called vibes. It is your behavior that projects onto your partner. Your emotions are transferred onto him, and he doesn't have control over his emotions and behaviors. Seeing you in such a negative light leaves him without options. He might be coping with his own insecurities, and need to become the image of calmness, security and peace that you want to see in your relationship.

It is very difficult to change unhelpful behaviors because they become habits, and as with any habits, it is easy to go back to them. But now that you have observed how those behaviors influence your partner and your relationship, you are aware that you need to change them. Focus on your values and the change will be much easier. Your values are what comes naturally to you. They are the morality that guides you through life. They are not something you think about; you feel them as part of you. You need to learn how to behave according to your values, not your emotions.

Do the Opposite

It will take a lot of energy to resist old habits and change your behavior to helpful ones, but as you practice and access new adopted behaviors, it will become easier. At one point, it will come without effort, almost automatically and naturally. This will make you feel better about yourself; it will be a great accomplishment. Instead of feeling unworthy, you will start to boost your self-esteem. Even your partner will recognize your effort and will reward you with even more love.

Let's look at some usual responses and behaviors you might have.

For example, you have abandonment insecurity and emotional deprivation core belief. You are dating your partner and you really like him. A situation happens at work that triggers your insecurities and you need reassurance; it's only natural to seek it from your partner. You call him, but he doesn't answer. You call him three more times to no avail. You start thinking that he doesn't like you as much as you like him; he is going to leave you, otherwise he would answer the phone. You start feeling anxious, depressed and scared, and you are already hurting. You have a strong urge to find out why isn't he answering right away, and you keep calling. He finally answers the phone; he is in a panic and asks what's wrong. You explain it's nothing, just something that happened at your job and your need to hear his voice. He then informs you that he was in the middle of meeting with an important client and your constant calling disrupted it. He hangs up. You feel bad about the situation and text him asking for forgiveness and say you panicked, and it is not your usual behavior. But it is; it is the behavior pattern you have when you feel insecure. Soon enough, your partner will have had enough and will want out of the relationship.

You seek unnecessary communication.

You need reassurance.

You are clingy.

You are in need of certainty.

This would be the helpful, opposite behavior:

Do not initiate communication and if you must, be sure you are not intruding on your partner's privacy.

Instead, do something to distract yourself. It could be a hobby, a quick exercise or simply organizing your work desk.

Instead of thinking about yourself, do something for a colleague, volunteer, or walk a neighbor's dog. Be helpful to others, shift focus from yourself to someone else.

Be aware of situations that trigger your insecurity. Stay in the present and don't give in to the traps of our minds. Meditate or have a relaxing cup of tea while contemplating your present experience. Remember, you have insecurities coming from your different core beliefs. Your situation might be different, but the steps you need to take to overcome it are the same as shown in the example. Be sure to use your personal values as guidance for helpful behaviors. This way, you won't feel like you are going against your nature and it will be easier to master newly adopted behaviors.

We humans continually adapt as social, mental, and physical beings. Just as our bodies reflect things like climate, food, and exercise, our spirits and psyches reflect our paths.

On the one hand, this adaptive ability allows us to manage future situations more effectively. On the other hand, it can keep us from taking on new opportunities. Our past experiences determine how we behave rather than seeing a person or circumstance as something different. Our memory ends with us, rather than the other way around. Maybe the best example is trust?

If a friend betrays us, when a business partner switches on us quickly, when a lover becomes unfaithful, our willingness to trust is shattered. The next time a friend makes a vow, a business partner proposes a project, or a lover asks us where we are, the error is assumed by our unconscious minds.

Even if we believe that everything is okay, our perception is clouded by the reminders of the past. Worse still, bearing this emotional residue will keep us from creating healthy new connections.

So how can we once again learn to trust? Can the words of the past be silenced? The solutions are more accessible than you could imagine. You can see people and situations through a more straightforward lens through regular practice and adherence to a few basic principles.

You have all the courage and strength to go through any challenges that occur in your life. You have a vast reserve of energy that you may not be sure of. You have the wisdom to know what you have to do in the situation in which you live. You can trust yourself to deal with what needs to be done. Confidence, confidence, and moving through every condition, one step at a time, will give you the trust and strength to move forward in your life.

If trouble or challenge comes in your path, when you are troubled and anxious, this is the time to put your trust in the Spirit, the Divine Presence, and to realize that now you can relax, knowing that God is in charge of it. You should trust and trust that everything will be all right.

At the right time and in the perfect way, our success always comes to us. Our life keeps rising in perfect timing. As we learn to believe and trust in spiritual peace, we find that we can let go and allow our lives to work for us. We are much more valued than we would have expected. God is Divine Wisdom and resides in each one of us. We always have that wisdom at our fingertips. Know now that God wants for us everything that is good and perfect.

Be mindful that the critical step in learning to trust is to look carefully at your own reactions. You don't have to criticize yourself or try to change your behavior. Only listen. What are the things you have experienced in the past? If you experienced mistrust, where does it come from specifically? Once past feelings surface, you will have a better understanding of why trust is hard for you. This perspective is going to inspire change.

Trust yourself. A great deal of mistrust of others stems from the incapacity to trust ourselves. The subconscious mind assumes responsibility when someone harms or betrays us. I was stupid enough to believe them. It's my fault. While it's true that we co-create our world, the reality is that many things are beyond our control. Forgiving and believing in our actions is a fundamental aspect of maintaining faith in others. Simple statements are a good starting point. In a reflective position, think, or say to yourself: "I trust in myself. I trust in my ability to make the right decisions. I trust in the world to lead me to where I need to go." Repeat such statements as often as possible using whatever terms and strategies suit you.

Find your natural state. When we trust life entirely, we know that we're on the right path. Yet our mental and spiritual powers don't always share this feeling. Restoring faith is a matter of linking our hearts and opening up in us the root of love. We instinctively want to feel satisfied, secure, and willing to trust others, whether in the bedroom or the boardroom. It may take compassion, validation, and good old-fashioned hard work, but it's really invaluable to be able to trust again.

CHAPTER 12
HOW TO HEAL YOUR ATTACHMENT WOUNDS

Heal your wounds, lower your armor, show your light.

If we have our 'armor' up and are mindful of our 'hurts,' we cannot show our light.

There are two essential doors to pass before we can understand our intellectual independence of mind, emotion, and spirit.

The first door goes against the grain of our human nature – to be sufficiently weak to lower the armor of our self-productivity.

But we must try to understand what we are covering before we can go forward.

Each of us, if we remove the protective armor, is gravely injured. The door to the true self is easily locked and fortified. No matter how amazing our parents were, they did not protect us from the hurts that cut our heart's sinews.

Every one of us has our past unresolved hurts and disappointments.

And it is the armored self that protects us.

However, the armored self is not always an ally. It often works against our best interests, because it is fueled by fear.

To become more of the person we are deep within – the one who lives free of spirit – we must cope with or at least be honest about our wounds.

We can't do this with our armor, so we have to remove it. But it must be said that it can be even more harmful if our wounded self is exposed to rolling attacks without the right preparations.

Because of this, we must build up stocks of courage.

Imagining an eagle soaring in the sky, wholly allowed in his flight, without fear. However, we're not like this so often. We're far less too many times.

Each of us is a divine being with the light potential that the whole universe will be captivated by. But first, our armed selves and wounded doors have to be opened.

It is not until we prepare ourselves with courage that the wounded self, will turn the armor into the truth and opportunities for development that prevail every day.

How to Heal Your Wounded Inner Child

When you permit your wounded inner child to live through you, you suffer the results of a damaged or blocked archetypal pattern. The injured infant makes reference to the broken emotional patterns of stressful experiences or events of childhood. You continue to experience the same negative experiences repeatedly as adult.

You confront the archetypal power in your psyche by healing. You challenge your inner child's voice instead of stifling it. Since you cannot turn the clock back, you take a number of symbolic gestures to show your inner child love and appreciation.

Here are some steps to cure your wounded child:

Understand the programming of your childhood. Any distorted self-images can be found in your childhood stories. Actually, your perception and relationship with others are greatly influenced by what happened in your youth. Do you need a picture?

The training of children is primarily influenced by their carers. When you were young, your caregivers represented the world to you. You look at them as examples of behavior. You then formed relationships based on what you learned from your parents and observed in them. Your parents learned from their parents in turn. So, you have built up layers of convictions, patterns, and behavior from one generation to the next.

Recognize life patterns repeated. At first glance, your experiences may not look like those in your past that traumatized you. Negative patterns, however, ultimately have the same emotional pain capacity. You must be able to recognize them in their different forms.

For example, a history of sexual abuse can result in your own children being abused by emotion. Rejection can be traced back to abandonment years ago. Anorexia, obesity, or depression can be traced to our younger parents' negative self-images.

Not many of us are brave enough to succeed in removing their childhood trauma. Instead, most of us are carrying our negative baggage. Every aspect of our lives shows the same patterns, whether with oneself, at home, or outside.

Recognize the pain. Your wounded child's needs have been stifled for the longest time. Healing the injured child allows you to recognize the trauma and damage you have endured. You understand that you are motivated to make many of your decisions, behaviors, and convictions because you had to avoid pain. It is essential to know that much of it is based on fear, and therefore does not serve you in your highest good.

Refrain from self-judgment. Do you judge yourself harshly? Realize that your childhood programming helped you cope with and navigate a confusing time in your growing years. Then you were a child. You had to endure the idea that the world wasn't very healthy.

Embrace the wounded child. This is an act of self-love. When you think about it, you realize you were forced to grow up too fast. Somehow, you have to leave the baby behind so you can cope with the speed of life. The kid you left behind never had the opportunity to play or be alive.

Though the past cannot be changed, you heal your injured child by making a symbolic gesture. You are now visualizing the acceptance and love of your wounded child. You also vow that you will not ignore your injured child's needs any longer.

Practice bravery. The idea of letting go of your childhood story may initially scare you. You have been connecting with your past for so long that you believe that without it you will be lost. You feel rage at your parents, your family, or your friends for the person you are now. You have someone to blame for your dysfunctional self.

Okay, you have to realize that your ego must stick to a shape, a plot. It's fact; the childhood story is a collection of ideas from the past. You can't hope to build a life of dignity unless you first release your allegiance to an old script. You must stop feeding a mentality that is "poor me." You must be bold if you want to move forward.

Forgive fully. You must forgive with all your heart. It's not only about redemption for oneself. You forgive everyone who contributed to the situation in which you now find yourself. Taking one or two steps back, you can see that your parents have also been influenced by their own childhood experiences. They have inflicted unwittingly on you what they suffered as adolescents.

When you find it challenging to practice full redemption, ask yourself if you want to remain in mental slavery. Mental slavery prevents you from constructing your worthy life. You can unstick yourself by taking control of your life from now on.

CONCLUSION

Were you thrilled to see that you are not the only person dealing with the feeling of insecurity? "Why would that make anyone thrilled?" you might ask. Well, the answer is simple: you're not alone. Never feel like you have to walk this world all by yourself without someone to turn to. In this book, we have seen how you can make the best out of all the relationships that you have, and how to avoid behaviors that might not help grow your relationships. Whether the person you turn to is a family member, a friend, or your partner, you'll be ready to leave your insecurities aside and be open to them.

Of course, being insecure in love has its challenges. Even your partner might not understand at times why you do certain things. But this doesn't mean that the obstacles are insurmountable. You can unlearn bad and harmful patterns of behavior and acquire new ones that will improve your relationship. Your partner will be very happy to see how much you can change. What is more, that change for the better shows how much you love yourself and him. Your love on display will certainly impress your partner.

You have seen how frank communication is necessary for a relationship to flourish and at the same time how you need to give your partner a measure of privacy. Find a balance between these two. Continue talking to your partner about your feelings, voice your opinions and thoughts. Don't forget that your partner also has a voice and so he will also convey his own ideas and opinions. When confronted with disagreements, treat him kindly and avoid assuming your partner has hidden motives. He understands that he also makes mistakes and is trying to improve like you are right now.

Learn to let go of the past. Focus on the present and on what lies ahead for the relationship. Realize that your partner is your greatest confidant. Cherish the moments you spend with him and you'll have a great treasure of memories to contemplate in the future.

Safety in a relationship is not to look back at what it was in nostalgia or to what it might be, but to live and accept the current relationship, as it now is.

Jealousy will ruin your relationships absolutely. Where does it come from, and what can you do? Relationships have four options: neither of you is jealous, you are envious but your partner is not, your partner is jealous, but you are not, or you are both envious. The first example does not stress the relationship, while the last three are stressful.

You are jealous, and your partner isn't, you don't know if you can trust the one you love. You doubt his or her actions and blame him or her, either openly or in your head. You have no confidence and offer very little, if any, privacy to your partner.

Your partner has faith in you. He or she won't bombard you with ten thousand questions about who you were and where you were. This is possibly perceived as evidence of how little he or she cares for you when the opposite is exact, in fact.

If your partner is jealous, but you aren't, your partner is nuts! He or she's going to smother you. You love your partner, but you can't breathe. He or she needs to be with you regularly, asks you questions about who you are with, and what you are doing, may want to check your cell phone and e-mail to see who you interact with, and does not necessarily trust you.

The first thing you have to remember is you can never change your partner. Many couples think that if they marry, the jealous partner will lose his fear. This vulnerability follows a person, regardless of marital status. If a person has a burning desire to change their jealous attitude, he or she must work hard to complete that, but a marriage certificate is not a cure for jealousy.

So ask yourself, is he still the one you want to be with if your partner never changes and maintains this jealous conduct forever? If the answer is yes, then you have to learn how to deal with the relentless doubt and intrusions in your life. If the answer is no, you must formulate an end strategy or at least decrease the amount of time you spend in the relationship.

In this case, both of you work either from the need for strength or from the need for life. You are either afraid to be alone or want to control the behavior of your loved one, which is not particularly healthy.

Your relationship could last for a long time. As you both work from the same place, you probably would not notice the chaos. Nonetheless, you need to be able to see what life would be like if you were in a relationship with your partner or someone else, and trust existed between you. You should know something stronger, and deliberately commit to action that generates that kind of confidence in your life.

When the problem is that one or both of you have been unfaithful in the past, then there are some real trust concerns. If you were the one who lied, try to grasp the fear and fears of your partner at least briefly. The person who has cheated causes his life to be an open book for his wife. In this case, enable your partner to access your comings and goings to help them develop trust again in your relationship.

If you were the one whose partner fooled around, you're not off the hook. If your partner gives you the opportunity to really know all the time what he or she is doing to restore confidence in you, you must also work together to regain faith. You must be open to the idea that your partner is making improvements and is really sorry for his indiscretion. You have to give up your desire to punish him or make him pay and really start rebuilding your relationship. Let your anger go and move forward.

Real love does not work on the principle of scarcity. To receive love, you have to give it freely. Trust is the only way to go if you love someone and want peace of mind.

Jealousy is like a disease that invades your friendship. It has the power to be devastating. Do not allow envy to erode your relationship's honesty, love, and respect.

Extending your faith and confidence is a gift to the person you love. If he or she is an honorable person, the reward is preserved, and well looked after. If he or she isn't, it won't be long before you discover the real character of your friend. And you're going to have a decision to make when you do.

Your jealousy is often perceived as something externally activated, but it's 100% internal programming in realistic terms. It can be daunting psychologically to understand what triggers envy, but there can be a systematic approach to understanding why you feel the way you do.

There are a lot of things that cause jealousy, as many individuals have found. Jealousy comes from low self-esteem or self-image. The underlying principle is that our whole universe is mediated by our filters of perception. If we have a bad image of ourselves, or if we do not feel strongly about ourselves, our filters are compromised. Everything we see on the outside is modified, and our emotional responses are incorrect.

For example, if we are profoundly addicted to the affection, love, and appreciation of our lovers but don't feel like we deserve it for any reason, then we start worrying about them leaving us or moving on. That understanding is just in our minds, and we like to analyze things and give them non-existent significance. Our own fear of them leaving us for a better-looking man lets us see every guy who we think looks better. A normal conversation leads to worry about the exchange. Anxiety occupies our heads. Jealousy is a symbol of our own fears and worries, and often we can create a self-fulfilling prophecy that we will lose the one we love and need.

While your lover is 100% dedicated to you, your acts of fear may frustrate her, and you may change her mind about what she thinks about you by your own actions. You tend to make her want to avoid the discomfort that your manipulation causes, and when she leaves, you only affirm your suspicions when it really just occurred because you did not deal with the emotions at their heart.

Jealousy can be repaired, ripped apart, and uncovered, but you must accept that it is a problem, and you must want to change it. You have to focus on the way you see yourself, your self-esteem, and your thinking or internal conversations. The real problem is inside.

It's important to realize that a relationship riddled by anxiety and insecurity doesn't have the greatest outlook attached to it. Whilst it's not always doomed to fail, it's not going to be a happy and close relationship; how can it be when your partner is always thinking you're doubting them and you're always reading into things? Being at the mercy of your fears won't make you happy, and if you want to ensure that your fears don't come into fruition, the best thing is to overcome them and simply live in the moment, enjoying your relationship for what it is, in the here and now.

There is no shame in admitting that you need help in this regard, and if you really feel like you have a past problem that is affecting you in the here and now, or you simply can't get past your fears, asking for professional help and assistance is a must-do. There is no failing or weakness attached to this, and it is actually one of the strongest things you can do.

There are many options for help and support but talking to your partner as the first port of call is a great idea. This helps them to understand what is going on inside your head and allows them the chance to try and help you deal with your problems at the source. In many situations, this is enough. If that doesn't work, there are other options, such as couple's therapy, individual therapy, and self-help methods to help you overcome anxiety. Your doctor may also be able to discuss medications with you if anxiety is a huge issue in your life generally.

Don't let fear win, don't let it derail your life for no good reason. Face your fears, overcome them, and look forward to a future free of constant relationship insecurities and anxieties.

Made in the USA
Monee, IL
23 August 2021